The SAVING POWER of SUFFERING

By Fr. Jacob Powell

Imprimatur:

Rev. Robert M Coerver
Bishop of Lubbock
February 22, 2023

Nihil Obstat:

Rev. William J. Anton
Censor Librorum

Cover image art by Mark Restaino

Paperback ISBN: 978-1-960410-09-2

"My God, my God, why have you forsaken me?..."
Psalm 22:2

May this book serve for the greater glory of God, the veneration of my Blessed Mother of Heaven, and the salvation of souls.

Contents

INTRODUCTION

"Then he said to all, 'If anyone wishes to come after me, he must deny himself and take up his cross daily and follow me.'"
Luke 9:23

Suffering is one of the most common human experiences known to man. It is an undeniable reality that affects every person regardless of age, wealth, education, race, or creed. Jesus himself told us that we would need to take up our crosses *daily* to follow Him, so why are we naively surprised when life isn't easy?

Part of our ignorance comes from the fact that most of us haven't been taught *how* to suffer according to Church teaching. Another aspect is that we see things from a human perspective and assume that a loving God wouldn't allow His children to experience pain and sorrow. When suffering inevitably occurs, we question God's goodness or wonder, "Why me?"

The pains of human existence have caused countless people to plummet into depression and fall into despair; yet they have also been the means by which saints have risen from the darkness of gloom to the heights of joy and peace. St. Thérèse of Lisieux, who suffered greatly, taught that "joy isn't found in the material objects surrounding us, but in the inner recesses of the soul" and that "one can possess joy in a prison cell as well as in a palace." Our perception and reaction to suffering is the difference between misery and joy.

Learning to properly view and respond to the sufferings of this life—and use them for spiritual progress—will prove invaluable throughout our years on earth. This book in no way promises to end suffering (something only God can offer), nor is it an attempt to replace confession, spiritual direction, or spiritual counseling, which are all extraordinarily valuable for healing. Rather, it attempts to enable us to more closely follow the footsteps of Christ. He is "the Way, the Truth, and the Life" who offers true joy.[1]

The good Lord desires that all His children reach peace—not only in the life to come, but even here, on our journeys toward heaven. How can we find peace when faced with the death of a friend, the discovery of a disease, or an accident? By reflecting well on Christ's life, we can come to the realization that even suffering has meaning and purpose. Jesus illuminates the road to peace, despite the potential problems along the way.

Suffering comes in a variety of forms. It can affect our emotional and physical capacities, such as mental or spiritual anguish, loneliness, insecurities, the loss of loved ones, rejection, and health issues. There are also the less obvious forms of suffering, such as unwanted lustful or blasphemous thoughts, distractions in prayer, elongated bouts of sorrow, or hardship in learning. *All types can be used for our sanctification.*

---

1   Catholic Biblical Association (Great Britain). The Holy Bible: Revised Standard Version, Catholic Edition. New York: National Council of Churches of Christ in the USA, 1994. John 14:6

Suffering truly can be redemptive, and you do not have to be a saint in order to begin using earthly hardships for good. God aids all of His children in using suffering to grow in love and in deeper union with Him. All that is required is to have the right perspective, to be in the state of grace, and to lovingly cooperate with His graces. This book is intended to open our eyes to this truth and help us accept whatever trials come our way—and even embrace them—as Christ embraced the cross.

It won't be easy; the American approach to any discomfort is to get rid of it as quickly as possible, numb it with pharmaceuticals, or suppress it, pretending it's not there. The Catholic approach to suffering and sorrow is certainly counter-cultural, but as St. Paul tells us in Romans 12:2, we must "not be conformed to this world, but be transformed by the renewing of [our] minds."

One of the main goals of this book is to shift our perspectives on suffering and align them with God's, in a way that fosters spiritual growth and brings us closer to Him. Here is a brief analogy to illustrate my point:

There is a chemical called dihydrogen monoxide that can be extremely dangerous. In his article *Dihydrogen Monoxide: Unrecognized Killer*, author James Glassman explains how this substance causes the death of thousands of people in America annually, is so caustic that it accelerates the corrosion of metals, and is even found in the tumors of terminal cancer patients. When someone develops a dependency on dihydrogen monoxide, withdrawal causes death. He then goes on to mention that this chemical is present in every river, stream, and reservoir in our country! Sounds pretty scary, doesn't it?

After hearing these facts, a majority of the people surveyed believed this substance should be outlawed or regulated. We can imagine their surprise when they found out the plot twist. Dihydrogen monoxide is better known by its molecular formula, H_2O. It is water!

Everything in the article was true. Water causes death, burns, corrosion of metals, and many other problems, but it is also essential for life on Earth and has countless benefits.

Just like with dihydrogen monoxide, most people examining suffering would choose to outlaw it or avoid it altogether because they misunderstand it and only see one side of the coin. They experience its sting and only pursue its terminus. If properly understood, they would realize the value of suffering and how enriching and salvific it truly can be.

This book will endeavor to show the other side of the coin. The *Catechism* tells us in paragraph 787 that "From the beginning, Jesus associated His disciples with His own life, revealed the mystery of the Kingdom to them, and gave them a share in His mission, joy, and sufferings." So as Jesus' disciples, we are privileged to share in His joys, His sufferings, and His mission, but what exactly does this mean for us? Within these pages, we will examine why suffering is a reality in this life, how to think of it from God's perspective, and practical ways to transform sorrow into a source of holiness.

If we take to heart what we learn here, we will not only benefit our own souls; we might help to save countless more along the way.

Jesus, we trust in you.

Hail, Holy Queen

*Hail, holy Queen, mother of mercy, our
life, our sweetness, and our hope. To
thee do we cry, poor banished children
of Eve; to thee do we send up our sighs,
mourning and weeping in this valley of
tears. Turn then, most gracious advocate,
thine eyes of mercy toward us; and, after
this, our exile, show unto us the blessed
fruit of thy womb, Jesus. O clement, O
loving, O sweet Virgin Mary.*
*Pray for us O holy mother of God, that
we may be made worthy of the promises
of Christ.*

PART 1

Seeing It God's Way

As we examine the topic of suffering, it is important to understand and appreciate how limited man's perspective generally is. God sees the world entirely and correctly. Man perceives so poorly the causes and effects of actions, words, and events. Because suffering is so difficult and undesirable, it often influences our perception. It skews our understanding of the world and impedes our perception of truth.

In general, suffering is considered the enemy of human existence. Whatever is necessary to alleviate pain, avoid suffering, and escape emotional anguish is frequently more acceptable than embracing the difficulty at hand. Once we accept that God is a truly loving God Who desires our good, then we can learn to abandon ourselves fully to His Will, accept anything He allows, and trust entirely that He provides everything necessary to heal, mature, advance, and find fulfillment. Obviously, this is easier said than done!

When the sun falls beneath the horizon, man's sight is changed, not lost. Ironically, in the dark we are able to perceive far greater distances than in the daylight. We see the numerous stars and certain planets only when the sun has sunk below the horizon. In the dark, the beautiful and distant elements of God's creation that are otherwise hidden from sight are exposed. Similarly, as the shadow of suffering infiltrates a person's experience, reality is altered, not destroyed. Man sees God differently in these moments. Through our suffering God reveals Himself to us in new and rich ways. Suffering is not the ultimate enemy — sin is.

When examining suffering, it is beneficial to begin with an analogy that reveals the significance of different perspectives: A very young child naturally trying to walk decides to pull himself up on a piece of furniture. He uses the furniture for balance as he is accustomed to do. The child then sees his mother only a few steps away. Of course, to the child the mother is the source of security, care, food, warmth, and comfort. In order to be near his mother, the child removes his hand from the furniture and clumsily takes his first step without aid toward her. Although he lacks confidence, balance, and leg muscle, he is successful. When the mother sees his success, she takes one small step backward.

From the perspective of the child, the mother is abandoning him. The source of his security distances herself in the moment of his greatest need. His muscles probably ache, and he may even have a light level of fear. Why has she abandoned him? The mother's perspective is radically different. She takes the step backward knowing that she is there to help at any moment. She is in complete control and the child is not in any significant danger. She takes the step backward because she wants the child to learn; she has his best interests at heart. He needs those muscles strengthened, that balance developed, and confidence built through practice, repetition, and even failure. She is training him, and this training is a form of love and help. On the other hand, the child's limited view fails to grasp this.

The first section of this book is about learning to see suffering God's way, by looking at it through our Father's eyes. Let's start by examining why we are in this "predicament," and to do that, we must go back to the very beginning...

CHAPTER 1

Why is There Suffering?

"Sin is the assassin of the soul."
St. John Vianney

The title of this chapter is a question that humans have been pondering for centuries, and there is a good chance it has crossed our minds at one time or another. If God is "infinitely good," as paragraph 385 of the *Catechism* tells us, why would He allow us to suffer?

To get to the root of this question, we must start with the basics. The basics, just like basic training in the military, aren't always easy, but they are essential to leading us where we want to go. Let's spend some time back at the beginning, shall we?

If we think back to our religious education classes, we can likely recall the short answer to this question – sin is the cause of all suffering. Most of us are also familiar with the story of Adam and Eve disobeying God after being tempted by the serpent in Genesis 2 and 3. They let doubt about God's intentions sneak into their hearts and wound up bringing the consequences of original sin onto all of us.

This wasn't how God wanted it to be. God created humans to live in perfect harmony with Him without any discord, suffering, or imperfection. However, Adam's sin destroyed this heavenly condition in which man was created. Sin destroyed the soul's relationship with grace and the preternatural gifts.[2] God once walked in harmony with man, but sin separated us from our loving Father. Furthermore, God's precious creation—His exquisite masterpiece of beauty and harmony—was split apart by man's sin. Man once ruled over the animals, plants, and other creatures, but sin created disharmony between man and Earth—the soil, the animals, the weather, etc.

Man was originally created with an ordered interior life, where he desired God above all things; however, sin put enmity within man's soul. Disordered desires (also known as concupiscence) impeded growth in virtue and increased our attraction toward sin.[3] Jesus warned of this internal disharmony in the Garden of Gethsemane: "Watch and pray that you may not enter into temptation; the spirit indeed is willing, but the flesh is weak."[4] Without grace, we tend toward sin like a rock to the bottom of the ocean.[5]

Sin has become so commonplace and easy to commit that many of us consider it simply a part of human life, and don't truly realize the weight that it carries. Only after this life will each of us come to fully grasp the damage and destruction that sin causes. Sin has

---

2   Preternatural gifts were given to humanity before the fall. They include immortality, impassibility, etc.

3   Virtue is a strength, a good habit of the soul. Building virtue is a most necessary part of the spiritual life and reaching human potential. Justice, Prudence, Fortitude, and Temperance are the four cardinal virtues.

4   Matthew 26:41.

5   Remler, F.J. *Why Must I Suffer*. Loreto Publications, 2003. pg. 5.

many repercussions that are both visible and invisible. Let's touch on a few of them here:

1. **Sin blinds us by darkening our intellect.** Sin inhibits man's ability to recognize God's effects and movements in creation. Sin makes it harder to know what is the right course of action in any given situation. The natural gift of reason remains, but it is clouded and disordered.

2. **Sin hardens our will, making it harder to choose what is right, even when the right decision is known.** Many Christians might not understand how it is possible for a person to support abortion, condone transgender ideology, and defend same-sex unions. Sin is the answer. It blinds people from seeing and reasoning even the most simple and obvious moral issues. A person might have an intellect that surpasses even the most intelligent individuals and yet still be blinded from right reasoning with relation to various moral choices. Sin opposes everything God created man to be. He created man to know Him and love Him within a holy relationship, but sin makes it harder for us to know God and love God. It also destroys our relationship with Him because sin is a turning inward to self and away from God or any other.

3. **Sin wounds our soul.** The wounds caused by sin can affect our relationships, choices, and spiritual growth. They can cause us to wrongly perceive another person's intentions or actions. Even small offenses can become infected and turn into resentment and hatred. Sin can convince us that God does not care about us or that God does not exist. In fact, it is sensible to believe that many who reject the existence of God—an existence which is so reasonable and logical—do so as a result of

some often concealed emotional or spiritual wound. The book of Tobit reads, "...but those who commit sin are the enemies of their own lives."[6] Although it is wrong to assume some particular sin is the cause of some person's disbelief or suffering, sin is ultimately the cause. The wounds a person has may also be caused by the sins committed against him by others. Both our own sins and the sins against us leave wounds which affect us daily.

4. **Sin is communal.** The clearest example of this is the first sin of mankind. The fall of Adam resulted in the damage and disharmony of all creation. Every single human person, with the exception of the Blessed Virgin Mary, has been conceived in sin since the fall. This should clarify the real damage of sin: it travels downstream. Sin affects countless people. For instance, a father who verbally abuses his wife wounds her deeply in various ways (e.g. her self-esteem, her trust, her relationships, etc.). These wounds affect how she treats her children, her friends, and her neighbors. The children who witness this abuse may begin lying about their father's problem. Their image of God as a loving Father will likely become distorted, and the emotional turmoil can cause issues with trust and communication in future relationships, including their marriages. Some of the children may even fall into the same pattern as their father, negatively affecting their children. This is just one example, but the reality is that all sin is like this to some extent.

We often consider sin harmless if it does not affect another person directly. However, this fails to rightly consider how limited human knowledge is regarding the countless visible

---

6   Tobit 12:10.

and invisible causes and effects which emerge from free will. Sin always affects others; it is the nature of sin. God created humanity to be linked together. Christ established the Church, a community, to continue His mission on earth. He desires each of us to be united to Him intimately and uniquely in and through the one, holy, catholic, and apostolic Church, "for just as the body is one and has many members, and all the members of the body, though many, are one body, so it is with Christ."[7]

Of course, each of us should have an intimate relationship with God, but it ought to be in union with the community, not separated from it.[8] The idea that a person can be spiritual but not religious is the notion that a person can follow God on his or her own terms without a community, without Sacred Tradition. This person interprets Sacred Scripture on his or her own, discovers the spiritual life without the help of others, and discerns God's will alone. This is terribly false and a form of spiritual suicide in that it rejects the very institution Christ founded for the protection and propagation of Truth, namely, the Catholic Church.[9] This false notion itself is an effect of sin which confuses the right order of things. God establishes order, unity and harmony; sin disorders, divides, and disharmonizes to the point of destruction.

---

7   I Corinthians 12:12.

8   John 17:20-21: "I do not pray for these only, but also for those who believe in me through their word, that they may all be one; even as thou, Father, art in me, and I in thee, that they also may be in us, so that the world may believe that thou hast sent me."

9   1 Timothy 3:15: "if I am delayed, you may know how one ought to behave in the household of God, which is the church of the living God, the pillar and bulwark of the truth."

5. **Sin naturally causes suffering.** The "rules" that God has for us are ultimately for our good. Therefore sin, or breaking those rules, naturally causes negative consequences. For example, the person who continues to commit the sin of gluttony to the extent of becoming overly obese is the cause of much suffering, especially if this condition eventually leads to an early death. The person's choices result in far worse consequences than physical discomfort, difficulty breathing, and other annoyances that accompany obesity. Rather, his or her attachment to the sin of gluttony may also result in a young widow and fatherless children. This suffering should not be blamed on God, but on the poor and sinful choices the person made. So much suffering is derived from the direct consequences of human decisions with relation to illness, venereal disease, war, broken relationships, and costly mistakes. Yet, God is still able to create good out of human weakness.

(Sin has many other effects besides the ones listed above, including spiritual damage and temporal and eternal punishment, but these will suffice for the purposes of this chapter.)

God disfavors sin because of the damage it causes; however, there is an even greater reason: sin is utterly opposed to God. God is perfect light; He is perfect justice; He is perfect Love; He is perfectly good. Sin is the opposite of this. All too often we question God because we are suffering, yet we fail to acknowledge our many offenses against Him. We fail to see in what grievous and pitiable ways we have rejected the God Who is perfectly just, loving, good, and powerful. How quickly a father grows impatient with his child who fails to obey immediately; yet, how often mankind has slighted God in small and big ways without much concern or contrition. Why are we allowed to get annoyed, impatient, or even upset at being poorly treated, but God is cruel if He ever acts justly toward humanity in relation to sin?

Nearly every person in the world commits at least one sin every single day. Therefore, considering the population of the world, humanity offends God at least eight billion times every single day. In reality, God is offended far more than this because the vast majority of humanity commits multiple sins daily. Think of all the murders, rapes, robberies, lies, gossip, fornication, self-abuse, usury, drunkenness, abuse, hatred, homosexual acts, false teachings, blasphemies, vanity, wrath, pornography, and adultery that occur in a single day throughout the world. How merciful God truly is! Yet, when we experience some form of torment or suffering, we have the audacity to blame God, as if He has abandoned His obligations. This is the tendency we ALL must fight.

Even a single mortal sin freely committed with knowledge incurs everlasting torment if the person who committed the sin doesn't seek God's mercy through the Sacrament of Reconciliation. Mortal sin is enough to reject everlasting salvation forever because of against whom the sin is committed. It is a rejection of the Almighty, eternal, and all-Holy God for the sake of some passing pleasure, some temporal good, or some perceived personal gain. Sin blinds us to God's grandeur and makes it easier to commit more sins.

After this life, God's immensity and glory will be revealed. It will be so clear why even the smallest sin is loathsome in His sight. A man who punches a stranger on the street is liable for penal consequences. A man who punches an officer on the street is liable for much worse penal consequences, because of the position of the officer. A man who punches the president is liable for even worse penal consequences, because of the dignity of the office of the president and his role in society. This is logical; yet, to extend this analogy to the eternal and Almighty God expresses to some extent the just consequence of sin. The more we strive to see reality according to God's view, the easier it is to accept all things and recognize how just and merciful God is in all things. Indeed, there is a danger in seeing things only from our limited perspectives, which are filtered and conditioned by society, personal bias, and past experiences.

The American mentality champions the importance of personal rights. This is not wrong in itself. Each individual does have certain rights which ought to be protected because they are given by God. However, the American mentality fails to appreciate the importance of the obligations which accompany every right. For example, the right to life is also an obligation to ensure every other person has the same right, all things being equal. This is of great importance in relationship to God. God has rights. He has the right to be obeyed by His creatures. He has the right to be respected and obeyed by the governments of the world. He has the right to be worshiped by His creatures according to His designs. Who now speaks of God's rights with relation to abortion, euthanasia, artificial contraception, in-vitro-fertilization, and many other forms of commonly accepted sins?

As there are consequences for the trampling of another person's right, there justly are consequences for trampling God's rights. Suffering is one of these consequences, which includes communal suffering, such as plagues, famines, wars, and natural catastrophes.[10] This is not to suggest that every form of suffering is a punishment directly related to a particular sin committed by the person who suffers. This is incorrect. It is unjust to recognize the plight of others and assume the kind or quantity of the sins which must have been committed. Many people who have never committed a single actual sin suffer immensely. Aborted infants, Jesus Christ, and the Blessed Virgin are examples. And many who have sinned little suffer inexpressibly. Several of the saints are witnesses to this truth. Their lives of holiness and devotion to God reveal how God's love and mercy are constantly at work in and through and above human frailty, calling every person to something higher.

When it comes to our own personal suffering, many of us blame God for the trials of our lives without giving any consideration to the devastating reality of sin, and where this all originated. The Sacred Scriptures are clear that the "wages of sin is death," but luckily for us, there is more to the story...

---

10   Expiation of national and public offenses against God is required to avoid many national and international punishments. As the Old Testament indicates, these punishments generally come after decades or centuries of idol worship, murder of the innocent, usury, homosexuality, unjust laws, common divorce, secular education of children, artificial contraception, common divorce...

CHAPTER 2

For God So Loved
the World

"For God so loved the world that he gave his only Son, so that everyone who believes in him might not perish but might have eternal life. For God did not send his Son into the world to condemn the world, but that the world might be saved through him."
John 3:16-17

As we established in the last chapter, the cold, hard truth is that we are all sinners who deserve death. Luckily, we are *loved* sinners. God loves us so much that He provided an escape from what we justly deserve.

1 John 4:9-10 says, "In this way the love of God was revealed to us: God sent his only Son into the world so that we might have life through him. In this is love: not that we have loved God, but that he loves us and sent his Son as expiation for our sins." God loves us so much that He sacrificed his Son for us! Many of us know in our minds that God loves us, but do we feel it in our hearts? Do we *truly* see Him as a loving Father?

Easily we can lose sight of God's goodness as mental, physical, or spiritual anguish arises. This tendency must be combated because recognizing God as a good and loving Father is essential to developing a good relationship with Him. It is also a necessary component of preventing suffering from becoming too heavy and transforming our sorrows into strength.

The more a person approaches God as a powerful tyrant, a cold despot, or a wish-granting genie, the more this false image affects prayer, growth, and a right relationship with Him. The reason the First Person of the Most Holy Trinity is rightly called Father by us is because God the Son revealed this term and name to His disciples in His ministry. Jesus taught: "Do not be like them [those who pray with many words but without love and devotion], for your Father knows what you need before you ask him. Pray then like this: Our Father who art in heaven, hallowed be thy name..."[11]

Remembering that God is a loving Father is so fundamental and valuable to properly guide us as we investigate the cause of sorrow. Thomas Merton, a Trappist monk, wrote,

> "It is only the infinite mercy and love of God that has prevented us from tearing ourselves to pieces and destroying His entire creation long ago. People seem to think that it is in some way a proof that no merciful God exists, if we have so many wars. On the contrary, consider how in spite of centuries of sin and greed and lust and cruelty and hatred and avarice and oppression and injustice, spawned and bred by the free wills of men, the human race can still recover, each time, and can still produce men and women who overcome evil with good, hatred with love, greed with charity, lust and cruelty with sanctity. How could all this be possible without the merciful love of God, pouring out His grace upon us? Can there be any doubt

---

11   Matthew 6:8-9.

where wars come from and where peace comes from, when the children of this world, excluding God from their peace conferences, only manage to bring about greater and greater wars the more they talk about peace?"[12]

We must not allow our sufferings to distort this proper perception of the Almighty God. When this good and loving Father created humanity from the clay of the earth, He chose to make us in His image and likeness.[13] In doing so, He separated us from all animals, plants and other non-rational creatures of earth. He created humans with the ability to think rationally and to make choices with the gifts of reason and free will. Genesis 1:27 is one of the first indications that God is loving. By giving us intelligence and free will, He demonstrated His desire to have a relationship with each one of us.

Reason is the faculty that enables us to understand and know not only things, but also each other. By reason, we communicate to one another by revealing our thoughts, knowledge, ideas, desires, past, and present situations through words, body language, and actions. Through communication, we are able to come to know each other more deeply. This is necessary for a growing relationship in love, because we must know before loving. Ideally, when we reveal ourselves to another, we draw the other person to ourselves by what we reveal. The other person then can choose to love. However, having the ability to love also means having the ability to choose not to love—to choose to put one's own good above another. Knowing should lead to loving. By the faculty of

---

12   Merton, Thomas. *The Seven Story Mountain*. Harcourt, Brace, New York, 1978. p. 128.

13   Genesis 1:27: "So God created man in his own image, in the image of God he created him; male and female he created them."

free will, we can choose to love—to desire the good of another not for our own benefits, but for the sake of the other.[14]

Although society expresses love as a passion or an emotion toward another, it is vital to understand that love is much more. The emotional component is real, but it is not the most important component. God is a loving God precisely because He is Love itself and because He desires our good. Although free will gives us the ability to choose the good (to choose God above all things), it also enables us to choose lesser goods over God (to choose our own desires above what is objectively correct and good). This is what Adam and Eve did in their sin; this is what we do when we sin. God did not create us to sin, nor to suffer. He created us to enjoy perfect glory with and in Him forever. However, this is only possible so long as we are free to choose Him in love. If this is forced, the relationship would not be one of love but one of slavery and coercion. If we lose touch with this reality, we are in danger of believing God to be cruel, careless, or indifferent when we suffer in this life. This can lead to the belief that God uses suffering as some kind of hammer to put us down. If we are to have any hope of reaching the proper perspective on suffering and finding peace in the midst of it, we must reject this notion.

Therefore, it is essential to realize that suffering is a natural consequence of human decision, not God's cruelty. Because we have free will, God *allows* certain things to happen. And because God loves us so much, He will sometimes use and send temporary sufferings to teach, punish, and correct His children, just as a father

---

14   St. Thomas Aquinas, STh I–II, 26, 4, corp. art.

disciplines his child.[15] As the book of Judith explains, God mercifully uses these sufferings for the good of our souls: "Remember what he did with Abraham, and how he tested Isaac, and what happened to Jacob . . . . to search their hearts . . . . the Lord scourges those who draw near to him, in order to admonish them."[16]

To acknowledge God as a loving Father insinuates the following realities of His relationship with mankind:

1. **God desires the good for humanity.** God desires good for each of us, not because of what He can gain from us, but because of what we can gain by and through Him. This is perfectly revealed in the Incarnation and Christ's tormenting death on the Cross. God so thoroughly desires the good and the salvation of humanity that He sent His only-begotten Son to offer salvation to all who would accept it.[17]

   God clearly is not a tyrannical God thirsting for humanity to suffer. He is radically unlike the false gods of the pagans who demanded the blood of thousands of innocent men, women, and children. God does allow people to suffer, but He does so for good reason (which will be discussed later).

2. **God desires to provide for His children.** To view God as Father indicates that He has a desire not only for His children's good, but also to provide all that they need to thrive. St. James taught: "Do not be deceived, my beloved brethren. Every good endowment and every perfect gift is from above, coming down

---

15   Sirach 30:11-13: "Give him no authority in his youth, and do not ignore his errors. Bow down his neck in his youth, and beat his sides while he is young, lest he become stubborn and disobey you, and you have sorrow of soul from him. Discipline your son and take pains with him, that you may not be offended by his shamelessness."

16   Judith 8:26-27.

17   John 3:16.

from the Father of lights . . ."[18] What father would refuse to protect or provide for his own children? Jesus said:

"For every one who asks receives, and he who seeks finds, and to him who knocks it will be opened. What father among you, if his son asks for a fish, will instead of a fish give him a serpent; or if he asks for an egg, will give him a scorpion? If you then, who are evil, know how to give good gifts to your children, how much more will the heavenly Father give the Holy Spirit to those who ask him!"[19]

God is not indifferent to human suffering, nor does He desire it without having a higher purpose for it in this life. Too often, people wrongly think God is like the boy with the magnifying glass who torments ants by using the heat of the sun through the glass to burn them—as if God just plays with human lives to overcome boredom. This is both a false and a blasphemous perspective, and it is spiritually destructive because it affects our ability to know God, love God, and receive God's graces.

God created man out of His goodness, because He desired to share with all humanity His everlasting and perfect glory. By creating man in His "image and likeness," He created humanity with a nature that only finds fulfillment in God Himself. In fact, God's goodness far surpasses even His generous creation of human nature.[20]

---

18   James 1:16-17.

19   Luke 11:10-13.

20   Nature can be understood by the qualities and perfections of a creature. E.g., the nature of a horse endows the horse with the capacity to run quickly on four legs, eat, drink, metabolize, reproduce, react by instinct...

Because we know that God is good, and works everything out for our good, suffering must be beneficial in some way.[21] We will explore these ways in the remainder of Part 1.

---

21   Romans 8:28.

CHAPTER 3

The Significance of God Becoming Man

"He took the nature of a servant without stain of sin, enlarging out humanity without diminishing his divinity. He emptied himself; though invisible he made himself visible, though Creator and Lord of all things he chose to be one of us mortal men. Yet this was the condescension of compassion, not the loss of omnipotence. So he who in the nature of God had created man, became in the nature of a servant, man himself."
St. Leo the Great

I t's important to understand that God the Father most perfectly manifested His love for mankind in the Incarnation of the Son of God, i.e. God becoming man. This mystery of the Faith is as beautiful as it is salvific. After humanity committed sin, the relationship between God and man was severed. Although God spoke to various persons of the Old Testament, the relationship was never able to be wholly healed. The demand of justice for sin against God is something man must pay, but only God is pure and perfect enough to do so. How can finite and imperfect creatures offer anything truly worthy of an infinite, eternal, and perfect

God? Who could give to the Father a sacrifice so valuable and precious as to be sufficient reparation for even a single offense against His majesty?[22]

Therefore, in a perfectly generous act, God the Father sent His only Son, the Second Person of the Holy Trinity, to provide a most dignified and worthy sacrifice to the Father on man's behalf. The Son of God is fully Divine in that He has the same Divine Nature as God the Father and God the Holy Spirit. He is one of the three Divine Persons of the Holy Trinity. Uniquely, when the Son is sent by the Father, He receives a second nature, a human nature from the Blessed Virgin Mary. Therefore, this Divine Person now has two complete natures, fully Divine and fully human. He is both God and man.

God has made Himself like us in all things, except sin. Saint Paul taught: "For we have not a high priest [Jesus Christ] who is unable to sympathize with our weaknesses, but one who in every respect has been tempted as we are, yet without sin."[23] This reality is the foundation to understand suffering. This profound and central mystery of the Christian Creed is essential to have the proper perspective of human misery. Jesus Christ is the bridge between God and man (who were separated by sin) because He is the God-man, Who has a Divine Nature and human nature perfectly united in His Divine Personhood. To summarize, the break in relationship between God and man was healed by the advent of the God-man and sealed by His suffering.

---

22   Reparation is the term referring to satisfaction made to God for our sins. Christ's Blood on the Cross is sufficient reparation for all sin. Those who accept Him through sincere repentance and cooperation with the grace of God are those whose sins are cleansed in His Blood.

23   Hebrews 4:15.

Some people may ask why it is that God allows so much evil and suffering. For instance, the heinous crimes against humanity by the communists and free-masons alone in the 20th century have caused incalculable sorrow. However, the sin of man, which is the ultimate cause of all suffering, is also made the cause of salvation by God's goodness. The Catholic Church cries out 'O happy fault' on the eve of Easter every year as She recalls that sin has merited such a glorious Savior. Without sin, man's glory never surpasses the perfection of the Garden of Eden. The new heavens and the new earth, where man and God are united through Christ, is a far superior reward. The human nature is elevated when God clothes Himself in it, in the womb of the Blessed Virgin. Thus, when Jesus ascends to His throne after His earthly mission is complete, God and man share the kingly throne in the God-man. To question God's care or calculation in allowing evil is to drastically fail to appreciate the ineffable splendor of Heaven promised to those who persevere.[24]

Christ came to win souls back from the dead. The ancient serpent lures many away from God through his cunning and persistence. He is the "roaring lion" wandering about seeking someone to devour.[25] Jesus came to save sinners and offer strength and truth, not to end human suffering and overturn all the effects of sin. It is no small point that Jesus Christ conquered the 'sting of death' through suffering.[26] He accepted every word of mockery, every look of scorn, every flagellation of hatred, every blow of condescension even unto death. He was tormented by His approach-

---

24   1 Corinthians 2:9: What no eye has seen, nor ear heard, nor the heart of man conceived, what God has prepared for those who love him,"
25   1 Peter 5:8.
26   1 Corinthians 15:55.

ing Passion which is made clear in the Garden of Gethsemane.[27] He suffered far more than what is imagined. His purity exceedingly heightened His Sensitivity to His anguish. He saw and carried all the sins of mankind. The agony of His soul far outweighed the terrible agony of His flesh. He suffered more than all other humans ever could or would.

If the Son of God is willing to suffer so profoundly in His humanity though He committed no sin and was not in need of redemption, then with His help, we certainly can accept our suffering. Indeed, we can even grow holier through our suffering. The death of Jesus Christ on the Cross gave meaning and value to suffering which it did not have before. He used His bloodied Cross to crush the devil's head. The measure of His sufferings makes visible His immeasurable love for humanity. The Savior transformed suffering by enduring it so perfectly. He transformed suffering by attaching it to His perfect love. He transformed suffering by using it as a tool to redeem humanity. He transformed suffering by allowing His disciples to follow in His footsteps. That is, He gives every follower the ability to use their own sufferings to attach themselves to His Cross.

He gives every follower the opportunity to resemble Him through suffering. By the amount of love with which we freely accept the trials of this life we are able to be like Christ. By offering our torments in union with those of Christ to the Father, we resemble the Savior in action and allow grace to conform our souls to His. The Navarre Bible Commentary reads:

---

27   Luke 22:44: "And being in an agony he prayed more earnestly; and his sweat became like great drops of blood falling down upon the ground."

"The way the Christian follows is that of imitating Christ. We can follow him only if we help him bear his cross. We all have experience of suffering, and suffering leads to unhappiness unless it is accepted with a Christian outlook.

"The Cross is not a tragedy: it is God's way of teaching us that through suffering we can be sanctified, becoming one with Christ and winning heaven as a reward. This is why it is so Christian to love pain: "Let us bless pain. Love pain. Sanctify pain.... Glorify pain!"[28]

The Cross is what converts suffering into salvation, tragedy into triumph, grief into glory. The heart of the Christian way of life is to allow the Holy Spirit to make us like Christ. He can use our sorrows to place us on the Cross with Christ.

Through baptism, our souls are united to Christ in a unique way which allows us to offer ourselves through Christ to the Father. Reflect well on the splendor of this truth. Because of Christ's humanity and suffering, we are able to be united to Him through grace and to finally offer worthy and dignified sacrifices to God the Father by way of union with the Son of God. So long as we, in the state of grace and for the love of God, offer our torments in union with the worthy and perfect sacrifice of Christ, that offering is perfected in the Blood of Jesus and truly pleasing to the Father. Because God became man, man is empowered to become like God and be pleasing to God because of the actions of the God-man. By becoming man and dying on the Cross, Jesus, through His human nature, gave us finite creatures the ability to repair our offenses against the infinite Creator. This is only possible by union with

---

28   *Saint Luke's Gospel*, The Navarre Bible (Dublin; New York: Four Courts Press; Scepter Publishers, 2005), 135–136. Josemaría Escrivá

Jesus because this union enables us to act like Christ and be conformed to Him.

Through the generosity of God, all men and women are invited to participate in this ultimate and everlasting Sacrifice of Jesus through the reception of the sacraments, which offer to us the grace merited by the Cross. When we respond to God's grace, which helps us accept our sorrows, our participation in the Cross of Jesus is deepened. In some way, we console the Sacred Heart of Christ.

Therefore, the death of Christ is the answer to so many of the difficult and heartbreaking questions that arise from the depth of the soul in suffering. Questions such as: Where is God? Why has this happened to me or my family, or why now? Why does He seem so distant? Why does He not care? Why does He not respond? Why does God not let me die instead of my child, my spouse, my friend...? The answer is Jesus Christ. God makes Himself so near that He becomes one of us. He shattered the silence and separation between God and man caused by sin when the Word of God became flesh.[29] "...Christ Jesus, who, though he was in the form of God, did not count equality with God a thing to be grasped, but emptied himself, taking the form of a servant, being born in the likeness of men. And being found in human form he humbled himself and became obedient unto death, even death on a cross."[30] If He manifests His love for man by His suffering, should we not also be willing to manifest our love for God by suffering? God uses suffering to purify our hearts and minds. Though it is a true

---

29   John 1:1-15.
30   Philippians 2:5b-8.

struggle, we can learn to open ourselves to this purification by accepting all that God allows.

The Cross of Christ is the very foundation upon which a successful view of human suffering is formed. In every other reason, point, or topic of this book, the redemptive suffering of Christ crucified must be considered. Nothing makes sense without this most magnanimous death. The death of our Savior is the prism through which we are to examine our own trials, and the paradigm by which we are to face our own difficulties. Human suffering remains an absurd enigma without the incarnation, crucifixion, and resurrection of Jesus Christ. "The Cross stands still while the world revolves around it."[31] We must let our worlds revolve around His passion and His resurrection. The death of Christ is the event at the center of human history; the Cross of Christ is the center of the world. When it is at the center of our hearts, we nail to that Cross all we do and suffer in this life. It is the 'Rosetta Stone' of human existence.

The stories of Scripture emphasize the radical importance of the Cross. In the time of the great Exodus from Egypt, the Israelites wandered for forty years in the desert because of their terrible sins against God. During this journey they began complaining once again about their hardships. Regardless of the numerous ways God supernaturally aided them through plagues against the Egyptians, the splitting of the Red Sea, the manna sent in the desert...they continued to only see their immediate difficulties and not the larger picture, the providence of God and His consistent care for them. God began to punish them for their wickedness by sending serpents.

---

31   'Stat crux dum volvitur orbis' is the motto inscribed on the obelisk in Saint Peter's square in Rome.

Several Israelites died from the poisonous bites. They repented of their faults against God and Moses. God gave them a solution after Moses prayed on behalf of the people of God. The book of Numbers relates: "Make a fiery serpent, and set it on a pole; and everyone who is bitten, when he sees it, shall live." So Moses made a bronze serpent, and set it on a pole; and if a serpent bit any man, he would look at the bronze serpent and live."[32] It may seem odd that Moses was ordered to make an image of the poisonous creature which was the punishment for their sins in order to offer the people a remedy. However, this story relates directly to the crucifixion of Christ.

The bronze serpent was lifted up in the desert before the people as a remedy to their punishment of death. The serpent externally resembled the creatures which were killing the Israelites; however, there was no poison in it. Looking upon this paradoxical image offered salvation for those sick and dying. The Son of God in His humanity was also lifted up. He was lifted up on a Cross for the salvation of the world. Here again, we find a paradox. Jesus externally resembled a terrible criminal, one who committed heinous crimes; He resembled a sinner. However, internally, Christ was absolutely pure and without any sin as the bronze serpent was without poison.

Everlasting death and the destruction of one's soul are the effects of sin. Looking to Christ crucified, with the eyes of faith and with the help of grace, allows the poison of sin and its effects to be purged from the soul as the poison of the serpents was purged from the bodies of the Israelites. Here again, the crucifix is the summit of human history in which everything else finds its purpose and proper order in relation to it. We all must live in the light of the crucifixion and resemble the wondrous love and self-gift of Christ

---

32   Numbers 21: 8-9.

in our actions. In our own suffering, we are to look to Christ crucified to see the nearness of God, the example of suffering well, and the love with which we ought to embrace our own crosses.

The Catholic Church regularly reminds all people of the significance of Christ's death in relation to each individual's suffering by the use of a crucifix found in a most prominent place in its churches. The cross is certainly an ancient Catholic symbol of salvation and the love of God; however, the crucifix, the corpus on the cross, is a reminder of God's nearness to humanity in suffering. The crucifix reminds every one of us to remain faithful in the midst of suffering. With the help of God's love, it reminds us that our sorrow can be the very instrument which transforms us into images of Jesus. This ancient symbol draws to mind the hideousness of sin and the significance of human suffering when endured and embraced for love of God. The entire theology of this book is visibly expressed in every crucifix. Though much prayer and reflection is necessary to draw out of the crucifix the treasured teachings of redemptive suffering, they are present. They are present to us if we allow our loving Father to reveal these treasures to us.

CHAPTER 4

God Wants Salvation For Us

"Everything comes from love, all is ordained for the salvation of man, God does nothing without this goal in mind."
St. Catherine of Siena

As our loving Father, God desires not only the good of every human person, but the highest good. He has made humanity in such a way to find fulfillment only in Him. Every person desires perfect peace and lasting joy; however, no thing and no other human person can offer this. God alone can satisfy the longing found in the depth of the human soul.[33] God has made each of us to share in His perfect glory forever.

Sin alone can separate us from this perfect fulfillment. Sin is the name given when a person pursues some thing, some pleasure, some other for its own sake, as if that thing or person could satisfy the human longing. God can allow the suffering which ultimately comes from sin for the sake of a higher good. It is far greater to

---

33 In fact, this is a form of evidence that God does indeed exist. If man has a desire that nothing on earth or in the material universe can satisfy, there must be another outside of and transcendent to the universe who can satisfy this longing.

suffer (little or much) in a way that turns us back toward God and corrects our course, than to stay on the path that was leading to everlasting torment. With startling words Christ teaches, "And if your hand or your foot causes you to sin, cut it off and throw it away; it is better for you to enter life maimed or lame than with two hands or two feet to be thrown into the eternal fire. And if your eye causes you to sin, pluck it out and throw it away; it is better for you to enter life with one eye than with two eyes to be thrown into the hell of fire."[34] Hell is a reality that is too often forgotten. Those who enter there are those who have chosen it for themselves. God constantly draws us away from this place of destruction and helps us to choose what leads to life eternal.

His actions and mercy invoke us to trust Him and pursue righteousness. Saint Peter clarifies:

> "Humble yourselves therefore under the mighty hand of God, that in due time he may exalt you. Cast all your anxieties on him, for he cares about you. Be sober, be watchful. Your adversary the devil prowls around like a roaring lion, seeking someone to devour. Resist him, firm in your faith, knowing that the same experience of suffering is required of your brotherhood throughout the world. And after you have suffered a little while, the God of all grace, who has called you to his eternal glory in Christ, will himself restore, establish, and strengthen you. To him be the dominion for ever and ever. Amen."[35]

By an all-powerful God, suffering too can be used to convert, strengthen and make perfect. C. S. Lewis once said, "God whispers to us in our pleasures, speaks to us in our conscience, but

---

34   Matthew 18:8-9.
35   1 Peter 5:6-11.

shouts in our pains: It is His megaphone to rouse a deaf world."[36] If everything is comfortable in this life, what will draw a person to the next? If God gives us everything we seek on earth regardless of our numerous sins, what makes us pursue God above all things? He loves us too much to alleviate every trial.

God sees how everything is tied together. The Catholic Church teaches that at the end of time, after the return of Christ and the final victory accomplished against the devil, the Final Judgment will begin. At this time, all the souls from Heaven, hell, and Purgatory will be gathered together for the sake of a universal revelation. Every person's sins and good works will be revealed to every other person.[37] Additionally, God will reveal how every single action and word affected people and generations down through time. All will understand how God worked through and in prayer, sacrifices, the Mass, suffering...and how He remained in control despite the countless sins committed by humanity. It will be revealed how He created good out of evil decisions.[38] Human history and all it contains concerning moral and immoral actions, thoughts, and words will be seen as connected and controlled within the hands of God. All human moral decisions will be seen like a river flowing down the mountain of time where everything is interconnected,

---

36   Lewis, C.S. *Problem of Pain.* 140.

37   Matthew 10:26: "So have no fear of them; for nothing is covered that will not be revealed, or hidden that will not be known."

38   Certainly, a common difficulty among Christians is to be able to look at present situations of trial as a potential form of benefit. We should strive to do so. Think how impressive and life-altering it would be to realize that every single form of pain or sorrow was given to you specifically for the sake of your benefit. This requires a firm trust until God's plans are revealed. Imagine how even the darkest moments of your life are meant to be the periods of greatest growth in the light of Christ.

governed, and directed by the Almighty. He never robs humanity of free will; yet, He is not limited by humanity's misuse of it.

In light of God's perfect providence and knowledge of all things, suffering ought to be seen as a form of mercy from God. He could simply leave the sinner in his turmoil and guilt without calling out to him. He could abandon the sinner to his own decisions without offering redemption, conversion, and salvation. The father who sternly warns the toddler who is reaching for the boiling pot of water on the stove acts rightly. The child may feel wounded by his father's tone and abrupt reaction, but the father speaks to the child in a way where he can realize the danger of the situation. The child is incapable of understanding all the terrible pain and destruction the boiling water would cause; therefore, the father must speak in terms the child can understand. Although it might cause the child temporary sorrow, the father's intention is to protect him. If suffering is treated as the enemy, something to be avoided at all cost, then the person will inevitably question God's motives or abandon Him entirely. With this reaction, suffering begins to harden the heart and poison the peace of the soul. However, if suffering is seen as a natural consequence to sin, a temporary form of punishment (in certain circumstances) and an instrument of God to lead us to conversion or to greater heights of sanctity, then it ceases to be an impediment to ultimate fulfillment and becomes a means to it.

Temporal Punishment

Salvation is not the only reason God allows certain amounts of suffering. Temporal punishment is a significant part of understanding God's providence which underlies all that is experienced on earth, including all forms of torment. The book of Tobit reads, "He will afflict us for our iniquities; and again he will show mercy."[39] The Catholic Church teaches rightly and in accord with Sacred Scripture and Sacred Tradition that one of the effects of sin is called temporal punishment.

The Catechism of the Catholic Church notes, "Venial sin weakens charity; it manifests a disordered affection for created goods; it impedes the soul's progress in the exercise of the virtues and the practice of the moral good; it merits temporal punishment."[40] Eternal punishment concerns everlasting damnation, which is earned by every mortal sin. However, Christ's death has purchased the necessary payment for this punishment. A good confession remits the guilt of the mortal sin and expiates the eternal punishment.

So long as we are, by way of the sacraments, united to Christ's death and resurrection, we are free from everlasting punishment due to our past sins which have been cleansed in baptism and reconciliation. This state of union with Christ's death and resurrection is called the state of grace because grace is the necessary gift which flows from the Cross through the sacraments to unite man to God. By way of this grace, we are made pleasing in the eyes of God, Who then resides within the soul. However, temporal punishment can still remain a debt even for the soul in the state of grace. This form of punishment is a limited punishment which can and must be paid by those who commit sins.[41] Temporal punish-

---

39   Tobit 13:5.

40   Catechism of the Catholic Church, Second Edition, pg. 450.

41   Luke 12:57-59: "And why do you not judge for yourselves what is right? Thus, when you go with your accuser before a magistrate, on the way make an effort to settle the case, or you may be dragged before the judge, and the judge hand you over to the officer, and the officer throw you in prison. I tell you, you will never get out until you have paid the very last penny."

ment follows sin as necessarily as a shadow follows an object in the sunlight.[42] The size of the punishment differs based on the sin, as the size of the shadow differs based on the object.

Nevertheless, every sin must be expiated in some way or another in this life or the next.[43] A common example may clarify: A boy who disobeys his father's order to not play baseball near the house finds himself in trouble when the ball shatters one of the windows. Rightly, he apologizes sincerely to his father. The love of the father for his son compels him to forgive the boy of his disobedience. Therefore, the relationship between the father and the son is restored. However, the window is still in need of repair. The father, desiring to teach his son responsibility for his decisions, justice, and the value of a dollar, requires his son to pay some of the replacement cost. Because he knows that the son can only afford some of the cost, he only demands ten percent of the entire cost to be paid by his son.

The father generously pays the remaining balance for the new window. This is very relevant to temporal punishment. Although mortal sins incur everlasting punishment, the Sacrament of Reconciliation entirely pays this debt by Christ's death being applied to the soul yet again. This is similar to the part of the story where the father forgives his remorseful son. The relationship is restored. Similarly, the Sacrament of Reconciliation is like pouring again the waters of baptism over the one who stands in need of the mercy of the Father. The relationship is restored; however, not all debt has been paid.

---

42   Remler, F.J. Why Must I Suffer. Loreto Publications, 2003. pg. 29.
43   Remler, F.J. Why Must I Suffer. Loreto Publications, 2003. pg. 13.

Every sin, both mortal and venial, has also the effect of temporal punishment. This form of punishment is something that can be paid by man with the help of God. This relates to the ten percent demanded by the father for the replacement of the window. Some form of consequence is demanded of the son by the father. God is both merciful and just. It is wrong to separate these two attributes of God as if they are opposed to each other. God is not merciful only some days and just other days. Rather, He is always both. God is just in that each individual who has properly repented does pay some form of justice to the extent that it is possible in relation to his sins.[44] Likewise, He is merciful in that Jesus Christ's death on the Cross is fully sufficient to pay all debts owed from sin. Therefore, when the Father applies the just payment of His only-begotten Son's death to His adopted children's sins, He manifests both His mercy and justice.

God simply requires that we participate in some measure of the debt owed. The measure required by God is a tiny fraction of the punishment deserved. Although some children may be furious at having to pay ten percent to fix the window, objectively they should be grateful for the mercy, justice, and generosity of the father. Many people who come across suffering in this life grow immediately furious with God as if they do not deserve any of it. This is wrong; everyone who is guilty of mortal sin is deserving of hell. For God to require such little payment should compel gratitude above all.

Additionally, a further investigation of this parallel reveals the generosity of the father even more. The boy is only able to pay ten percent of the cost because the father gives his son an allowance

---

44   Romans 2:6: "For he will render to every man according to his works."

every week after having finished his chores. Although the son owes due honor and obedience to the father by virtue of natural law, the father desires to shower the child with gifts while also teaching him the value of hard work. In other words, the father does not really owe the child anything for the accomplished chores because the child rightly owes this work to the father; however, generosity leads the father to give an allowance anyway.

In applying this idea to temporal punishment, even the payment of the temporal punishment by one who has committed sins is only possible with God's help. Like the child who depends entirely on the generous allowance from the father, so every single human person is incapable of paying even a small amount of the debt owed due to sin without God's help. We are completely dependent on Him. All grace necessary for salvation, good works, and restitution of temporal debt comes originally from the Cross. Nothing can be merited entirely by man apart from God. Rather, Christ has merited everything, yet He desires like the generous father, to shower His flock with graces that enable us to pay all temporal punishment and store up "treasures in Heaven."[45]

Suffering is a form of punishment for sins committed; however, we do not actually reduce temporal debt without God's help.[46]

---

45   Matthew 6:19-20: "Do not lay up for yourselves treasures on earth, where moth and rust consume and where thieves break in and steal, but lay up for yourselves treasures in heaven, where neither moth nor rust consumes and where thieves do not break in and steal." "It is a fundamental teaching of Holy Writ [Holy Scripture] that the reward in the next world is proportional to the merits or demerits of life on earth." Fundamentals of Catholic Dogma. Ludwig Ott. Pg. 474.

46   Through the merits of Christ satisfaction is rendered to God for the temporal punishment due to forgiven sins by the patient bearing of punishments imposed by God, as well as by voluntarily undertaken penitential works, such as fasting, prayers, almsgiving and other works of piety. - Canon XIII in the 14th Session of the Council of Trent.

When we are in the state of grace and accept our sufferings and unite them to the sufferings of Christ, as a sacrifice to the Father, we are paying off our debt. We make reparation for past sins and further open ourselves to God's activity. This can only be done by grace and strength from God. Lovingly offering our sufferings in union with those of Christ to the Father requires the action of the Holy Spirit working in our souls. Therefore, as the son can only pay with the allowance given by his father, so we can only remit our temporal debt by the graces that were merited by Christ and given by the Holy Spirit.

To suffer does not bring us closer to God nor pay any amount of temporal punishment on its own. To suffer *humbly* in the state of grace and to unite *lovingly* every bit of it to Christ's death and Resurrection as a pleasing sacrifice to the Father is to cooperate with God's grace, be purged of imperfections, grow in holiness, and pay off some or all of the debt incurred from sin. We cannot offer God a pleasing sacrifice without His help. Jesus Christ's sacrifice on the Cross is the ultimate and perfect sacrifice in that He is the perfect victim (absolutely sinless and without imperfection) offered, and He is the perfect priest Who offers Himself to the Father. Therefore, every person who hopes to offer a pleasing sacrifice or gift to God can only do so by way of the merits of Jesus' death and by uniting one's self to His sacrifice. This is how suffering becomes truly redemptive for individuals. This is precisely how every individual should view and treat his own sufferings.

Temporal punishment, as has been shown, can be paid here on earth. While one is journeying to Heaven, any and all good acts done in the state of grace, through cooperation with the Holy Spirit and for the love of God are effectual in remitting temporal punishment. This again indicates God's overwhelming generosity. However, for the person who dies in the state of grace without having paid all the due temporal punishment, Purgatory is the first stop before entrance into Heaven. To die in the state of grace is to die in union with God. This union will continue forever after, but it will only be perfect after all imperfections have been entirely purged from the soul, for nothing unclean or without perfection is admitted into Heaven.[47] Temporal punishment is one of these imperfections that prevent a soul from entering the glories of Heaven immediately following death.

It is of great interest for every Christian to strive to pay all the temporal punishment here in this life before death. Numerous saints, holy authors, and stories of apparitions from souls in Purgatory, all agree that the lightest torments of Purgatory far surpass all the degrees and worst kinds of anguish on earth. Saint Catherine of Genoa and others also attest that the souls in Purgatory experience a far greater suffering, and at the same time a far greater joy, than exists in this world.[48] Both are caused by the far superior knowledge of God's perfections, love, and grandeur. This knowledge clarifies for the soul that fulfillment lies in God alone. Therefore, the soul thirsts to belong entirely and only to God in all ways. This thirst is a source of intense sorrow and anguish for those who must wait until their final perfection is achieved through the torments of Purgatory.

---

47   Revelation 21:27: "But nothing unclean shall enter it, nor anyone who practices abomination or falsehood, but only those who are written in the Lamb's book of life."

48   *Treatise on Purgatory* by Saint Catherine of Genoa is a short and powerful work which reveals Purgatory as a gift from God and a proof of His merciful love for souls.

Moreover, this thirst is a source of intense joy because the soul is nearer to God than ever and has the promise of future glory. All souls that enter Purgatory will enter Heaven. Purgatory, then, should also be considered a mercy from God because without a place of final purgation, nobody except those who are fully perfected, fully devoted to God, fully filled by God in all parts of the soul and in all ways could enter Heaven. Nothing even minutely imperfect can enter before the Face of God; therefore, if Purgatory was not created for those who die in God's grace but without having reached absolute perfection, Heaven would have far fewer souls and hell would have far more. Even in man's most intense sorrow, God's mercy is visible for those who have the appropriate perspective. Because the torment is drastically more intense in Purgatory, every person should use the sorrows, the pains, the annoyances, and discomforts of earthly life to remit all temporal punishment before death. Nearly all of the apparitions of our Lady to the children of God, in various locations and generations throughout history, encourage making acts of reparation for sins. The good works we perform and the suffering we humbly accept, for the purpose of remitting temporal punishment, is known as penance.[49] How much less despair and depression, apostasy, and suicide there would be if people understood how every form of pain or sorrow is a valuable opportunity for penance.

In every act of penance, we manifest to God our contrition for all offenses and for our desire to sin altogether. The Holy Water that flowed from Christ's Most Sacred Heart is the holy water of

---

49   Our Lady of Fatima revealed to the three children: "Sacrifice yourselves for sinners and say often to Jesus, especially each time you make a sacrifice: O Jesus, it is for love of You, for the conversion of sinners and in reparation for sins committed against the Immaculate Heart of Mary."

Baptism used to cleanse sin from the soul. Yet, in an astounding show of love, Christ allows each of us to pour this holy fluid again and again over our own souls in order to cleanse our temporal punishment through acts of reparation. He enables us to act with God in wiping away the debt owed from sin by cooperating with the graces that nudge us toward penance. Accepting our own suffering is one of the greatest forms of penance offered to man. This includes *every* form of suffering whether it be emotional, mental, spiritual, or otherwise. Through humble acceptance, we embrace God's Will above our own and manifest a trust and surrender to God in all things. We put into action our internal preference for God over comfort, God over personal desire, God over self.

CHAPTER 5

Treasures in Heaven

"Do not store up for yourselves treasures on earth, where moth and
rust consume and where thieves break in and steal; but store up
for yourselves treasures in heaven, where neither moth nor rust
consumes and where thieves do not break in and steal. For where
your treasure is, there your heart will be also."
—Matthew 6:19-21

God is desirous to reward His children and give them a greater share of His glory in paradise. God desires the salvation of all; however, not all are saved because He does not force anyone to accept salvation.[50] Everyone who is rewarded with eternal life is at a different level of perfection according to his deeds. God desires not only to save man, but to give him various rewards in relation to the grace he received on earth. Those in Heaven are not all enjoying the same level of glory. All are perfectly happy. All are perfectly fulfilled. However, the person who repents on his death bed having lived decades of sin and self-indulgence is not rewarded in the same way as the person who has striven for decades in sacrificial self-denial and obedience for love of God. Both are filled with

---

50   1 Timothy 2:3b-4: "...God our Savior, who desires all men to be saved and to come to the knowledge of the truth."

God's glory in unimaginable ways, but not equally. Although both experience the Beatific Vision, which is to see God as God sees Himself; they do so in different degrees.[51] The common analogy to clarify this distinction is to think of two cups of different sizes. Each of the cups are filled to the brim, so both are full yet the larger cup obviously contains more than the other.

God uses suffering as an opportunity to fill with greater heavenly reward those who accept it humbly. The loving Father even uses punishment to bless His children. God has a particular height and degree of glory He desires for each individual who will enter into Heaven; the graces, opportunities, and gifts He gives during one's earthly life is directed at helping the person to reach that position in Heaven. Suffering is a significant component to storing up rewards in Heaven. Saint Mary Magdalen de'Pazzi said, "You will be consoled according to the greatness of your sorrow and affliction; the greater the suffering, the greater will be the reward."[52] Like the martyrs who are crowned with celestial beauty and vestment that indicates the heroic testimony they bore for the sake of Christ, so those who suffer much in this life in the fashion of Christ, Who bore so patiently and lovingly His torments, will be rewarded forever after in a way that indicates the courageous ways they carried the extravagant weight of their crosses.

These celestial rewards are earned only in a certain way by the Christian. Christ is really the only One Who has fully merited the grace necessary for salvation, sanctification, and heavenly reward.

---

51   The Beatific Vision is to see God perfectly with the eyes of the soul. Man is created for this vision and can only find perfect peace and joy with it. The Beatific Vision is Heaven.

52   Second Letter of St. Mary Magdalene de Pazzi. The letter was addressed to a nun of St. Giovanni of the Knights of Malta.

However, He allows us to be saved and merit reward by cooperating with the grace given through the Holy Spirit. A relevant analogy: A father who is more than capable of picking an apple for his child allows his child to participate in the work. Instead of picking the apple himself, the father lifts the child on his shoulders and walks him to the nearest apple. The child then plucks the apple from the tree. In reality, the father did basically everything; the child merely cooperated with the work of the father. Yet, the child did participate. Rightly, one can say that he earned the reward of biting into the delicious fruit.

Concerning everlasting reward, Christ merits it all, but He allows man to participate by providing him with life, the opportunity to suffer, and the grace to suffer well, which originally was earned by His death on the Cross. All man does is comply and cooperate in love. This alone can be exceedingly difficult in our weaknesses, regardless of the fact that God has done nearly everything. This cooperation leads to more sanctifying grace, which directly and proportionately relates to the amount of heavenly reward we receive after this life. When we have cooperated well, God blesses us immensely and forever. This is evidence of God's justice. To say God is just is principally to speak of Him as One who desires to reward generously.

Reflection upon this truth only illuminates more the grandeur of God in relation to His care for humanity. He is the loving Father who uses suffering caused by our sins as an instrument and means to give us even greater perfection and glory in Heaven. The Christian who perceives suffering correctly, sees it not as an undeserved curse or a pointless scourge but as an opportunity for lasting rewards that far outweigh the quantity and length of the difficulty. How much the athlete is willing to endure for the sake of victory, how much more then should every person be willing to endure for the sake of purification of the heart, payment of temporal punishment, to resemble Christ more closely, and to accumulate heavenly rewards in abundance.

The apostles understood this notion as they suffered for Jesus: "So they [Sadducees] took his advice, and when they had called in the apostles, they beat them and charged them not to speak in the name of Jesus, and let them go. Then they left the presence of the council, *rejoicing* that they were counted worthy to suffer dishonor for the name [of Jesus]."[53] The grief of earthly life is passing; it has an expiration date. I know it can be tormentous and seemingly inescapable, but hold firm to the grace of God and allow Him to convert these present trials into the lasting jewels of your heavenly crown. Father Remler writes, "sanctify them [sufferings] by uniting them with the bitter passion and death of Our Lord, converting them into sources of rich supernatural merit, which in turn will procure for us in Heaven a throne far more glorious and exalted than if we had not fallen in Adam from the state of our original perfection."[54] How bountiful is God to enable man to do something here and now which echoes into eternity. How magnanimous He must be to give everlasting reward for a passing work of love.

---

53   Acts 5:41 (italics added for emphasis)
54   Remler, F.J. Why Must I Suffer. Loreto Publications, 2003. pg. 8.

CHAPTER 6

Service to Others

"When it is all over, you will not regret having suffered; rather you will regret having suffered so little and suffered that little so badly."
—St. Sebastian Valfre

The model manifested in the Passion and death of Jesus expresses the power of suffering. That is to say, the Savior used His sufferings as a remedy for the conversion of the world. His death is certainly the only reason salvation is possible, but His merits on the Cross are also the graces poured out onto individual souls for conversion and sanctification. Therefore, the soul who lovingly endures hardships and offers them in unity with the sufferings of Christ also merits grace for the sake of others. There is much power in our suffering when we generously offer our sufferings up for the atonement of the sins of others or for the conversion of another. Like many saints, St. Mary Magdalene de Pazzi modeled this behavior by often praying that God might send her infirmities and trials "to expiate the sins and procure the salvation of sinners."[55] God enables His adopted children to uniquely re-

---

55   Isolert, Antonio. The Life of St. Mary Magdalen de Pazzi: Florentine Noble, Sacred Carmelite Virgin. 1900 Philadelphia. 183.

semble His only begotten Son by embracing their crosses for the sake of others.

The parent who is anxious and guilt-stricken by the son's renunciation of the faith is generally unaware that the very sorrow caused by that renunciation is precisely what the parent ought to offer for conversion. Any and all suffering borne well and in the state of grace is salvific. If Christ's suffering is the source of all grace and all salvation, then it only makes sense that anyone who unites suffering to Christ's is also participating in the conversion and salvation of others. It is Christ who saves, nobody else; however, He desires that others participate in His salvation. This is clear when He started a Church in Chapter 16 of Matthew. It is clear when He sends out His apostles to preach and teach the good news.[56] It is clear when He gave them the power to bind and loose, which is a power to make decisions on earth that affect Heaven, in Chapter 18 of Matthew. It is very clear when He confers upon the apostles even the power to forgive sins.[57] The power to heal, preach, forgive sins, baptize, and help others to know and love God is always entirely from Christ. No apostle ever had any spiritual power outside of what Christ gave.

In a similar way, when we participate in the conversion of another by offering our sufferings for their sake, it is a fuller participation in what Christ has done for the salvation of the world. Suffering for the person while separated from Christ is without

---

56   Matthew 10:6-7: "but go rather to the lost sheep of the house of Israel. And preach as you go, saying, 'The kingdom of heaven is at hand.'"

57   John 20:21-23: "Jesus said to them again, "Peace be with you. As the Father has sent me, even so I send you." And when he had said this, he breathed on them, and said to them, "Receive the Holy Spirit. If you forgive the sins of any, they are forgiven; if you retain the sins of any, they are retained."

supernatural merit. God's grace in us is necessary, because without His grace we are without Him. Suffering to atone for another's temporal punishment, conversion, or spiritual growth while bound to Christ in grace is significantly useful and truly pleasing in the eyes of God.

It may be beneficial to return to the analogy of the father who allows his son the ability to pick the apple. The father wants to pick an apple not for his son this time, but for his spouse. Again, the father has all the ability to do so; however, he allows his son to participate. His son, carried on the father's shoulders, plucks the apple from the tree and gives it to his mother. The reality is that the father was the only necessary character to satisfy the hunger of his spouse. Yet, rightly the child can say that he plucked the apple.

St. Thérèse of Lisieux is a stunning role model in this regard. She recounts in her own autobiography how after Mass one Sunday in her youth she was pierced with a powerful thirst for souls when an image of our Lord's pierced hand slipped partially out of her book. She recounts: "From that day the cry of my dying Saviour— "I thirst!"—sounded incessantly in my heart, and kindled therein a burning zeal hitherto unknown to me. My one desire was to give my Beloved to drink; I felt myself consumed with thirst for souls, and I longed at any cost to snatch sinners from the everlasting flames of hell."[58] She then heard that an infamous criminal named Pranzini was sentenced to death. She fervently prayed with great confidence in the mercy of God. Although Pranzini originally rejected confession and absolution from the priest, he did turn back on his way to the scaffold and kissed the wounds of Christ on the crucifix which the priest held out to him. Her prayers and sacri-

---

58   Lisieux, St Therese. *Story of a Soul.* Paragraph 56.

fices were not without merit. This was the first of the sinners who benefited from the holiness of young St. Thérèse.

Likewise, God treats us with such munificence. He is the only One Who can save, but He allows others to participate in the salvation of sinners and the expiation of the effects of their sins.[59] This allows Him to give even more heavenly reward. Mary conversed with Sister Lucia, one of the three visionaries of the apparitions in Fatima, Portugal:

> Mary: "Do you wish to offer yourselves to God to endure all the sufferings that He may be pleased to send you, as both an act of reparation for the sins with which He is offended and an act of supplication for the conversion of sinners?"
>
> Lucia: "Yes, we do."
>
> Mary: "Well then, you will have much to suffer. But the grace of God will be your comfort."

How blessed Heaven will be for the souls who arrive and discover that their loving acceptance of the cross benefited several other people.

Atoning for the sins of others is an opportunity granted in two ways. Firstly, as mentioned above, a person can willfully accept his grief and offer it for the expiation of the sins of others still journeying toward the life to come. In doing so, he helps that person toward conversion of soul and to avoid Purgatory after this life. However, the souls in Purgatory are also able to enjoy the benefits of our cross embracing. We benefit from their prayers

---

59   Can you imagine how remarkable it is at the moment of death, a person who is poorly disposed to seek forgiveness for his sins is aided when the Mother of God pours out the lovingly accepted sufferings of her children on the soul of the one in need? These graces soften the heart and offer one last opportunity for redemption.

of intercession, and they are benefited by the prayers and acts of love performed by those on earth. They are our brothers and sisters. These souls must be a principal priority for all Christians who have not yet encountered death. Often the souls in Purgatory are forgotten in contemporary Christian conversations.

When we lose a loved one, we tend to think the person is in a better place. Although hope must be a firm reality for every Christian, his ability to help the deceased very possibly remains in his power. Once a person has entered Purgatory, he is incapable of helping himself. Only on earth can we make atonement for our own sins or the sins of another. Therefore, the souls in Purgatory are directly dependent on the prayers, sufferings, and works of mercy of their brothers and sisters on earth. They are closer to Heaven than us; yet, they experience profound torment in their final preparation for Heaven.

If a soul could reappear to his loved ones, he would plead for their grief, sorrow, and trials to be used as a cooling water to dull the sharp bite of the flames of Purgatory. Fr. Remler posits,

> "Supposing the dead could come back to make a personal appeal to their friends what do you think they would say to them? Would it not be something like this? 'If you truly love us, away with your immoderate grief, with your tears and wails which bring us no relief whatever! Away with these floral decorations, and these expensive funeral customs, which are more pagan than Christian and do not afford us any relief whatsoever. Help us by your prayers and good works, and above all by perfect resignation to the adorable will of the Author of life and death. All that we crave is speedy deliverance from our

frightful torments, and an early admission into Heaven. Prove your love by procuring for us this precious boon."[60]

If people really would only believe in this reality, they would find their reaction to loss very different.

Psychologically, helping another person is very healing and beneficial. We still can help so many who have gone before us. God has made the Church in a way where death cannot even prevent a soul on earth from helping a soul in Purgatory. Using the tears and sorrow which come from the loss of a loved one to expiate any temporal punishment he or she suffers in Purgatory also benefits the one who offers the sufferings. This symbiotic and mutually beneficial act of love reveals the transformative power of love as it encounters pain and loss.

---

[60]   Remler, F.J. *Why Must I Suffer*. Loreto Publications, 2003. pg. *42*.

CHAPTER 7

The Other Side of the Coin

"The more you are afflicted, the more you ought to rejoice, because in the fire of tribulation the soul will become pure gold, worthy to be placed and to shine in the heavenly palace."
—St. Padre Pio

T he previous chapters in this section have reminded us that suffering entered the world because of sin and demonstrated how God's love and Jesus' sacrifice allow us to use suffering for good. We've discussed how God wants salvation for us, allows us to store up treasures in Heaven, and lets us use our suffering to help other people (including the poor souls in Purgatory). Now that we've gotten a glimpse of the other side of the coin, let's look at how these various factors apply to particular situations. The following are a few examples not intended to be actual reasons for the sorrow and pain that arise from common conditions, but simply potential reasons to consider in order to broaden our limited human perspectives:

1. Perhaps stubbing our toes is an opportunity for us to remember how terrible must be the pains of hell and a reminder to pursue God in all things. All suffering should offer this reminder. All persons who have committed sin are deserving of

everlasting separation from God. Therefore, all anguish should inspire greater gratitude to God, whose mercy even now prevents the flames of hell from consuming many who still have the opportunity to repent and live by the truth of the Gospel.

2. Perhaps the death of a loved one is a mercy from God Who knew that person would have later fallen from Faith and rejected salvation. It is infinitely greater for that soul to have died earlier in life in a state of grace than later in a state of sin. Perhaps at the time of his death, his disposition was such to make a good repentance and cooperate with God's grace to make an act of perfect contrition.[61] Or perhaps this person is in a less terrible and tormentous area of hell resulting from less sins committed because of a shortened life. Although this is not an easy example to consider, it still can broaden the limited view of mankind and provide an answer where often no answer is found. Regardless, Christians should maintain a reasonable and true hope in God's mercy with relation to the salvation of loved-ones until all related answers are revealed after this life.

3. Perhaps, the cancer patient is suffering so immensely because of the temporal punishment owed due to his sins. Perhaps that patient will be able to avoid much anguish in Purgatory as a result of this temporary earthly suffering, so long as it is accepted for love of God.

---

61   An act of perfect contrition is the extraordinary means by which God, Who gives the grace to certain souls, helps a person in the state of sin repent wholly for sorrow for having offended God. In other words, perfect contrition is sorrow for sins not borne out of fear from suffering and punishment, but purely for love of God.

4. Perhaps, God allows us to feel as if He is absent from us to encourage us to pursue and desire Him more fully. Spiritual indifference is often overcome as a result of some form of torment. Dryness in the spiritual life often purges us of any selfish intentions concerning our desires for God. Sometimes, we begin seeking the consolations which come from God instead of seeking God Himself. Dryness can remedy this if we are willing to accept the difficulty and remain consistent in prayer and sacrifice.

5. Perhaps the emotional torment of a crumbling marriage is precisely what God will use to heal the marriage so long as one of the spouses embraces those sufferings and unites them with Christ's. So much good has resulted from the many tears shed on behalf of another who is in need of conversion.

6. Perhaps the child who suffers rejection and is the victim of bullying will develop the virtues of generosity, kindness, and patience as a result of the suffering. In other words, God might use that situation to prepare that person for much harder trials to come. Or, perhaps those virtues developed will be the soil from which a true and lasting friendship will blossom in the future.

7. Perhaps that child who suffers and dies from cancer is the source of torment for so many who eventually grow more faithful, more Christ-centered, and humbler. Although a person might reject this potential explanation, one must remember, sin is the source of suffering, this life is temporary and so short compared to eternity. What is two years or 80 years of torment in light of everlasting peace and numerous more celestial rewards. If God offers rewards, blessings, and perfect

peace that far surpass human imagination and experience, then why should we use our own suffering or that of another to blame God, hate God, or deny His existence? Certainly the intense emotional reaction of a parent in this sort of situation is impossible to fully grasp by one who is not in it; however, this does not change the fact that God is greater than our most difficult hardships; God offers grace to make even the worst things good; God is provident and desires the ultimate good of every person directly and indirectly involved. Perhaps God knows better. Certainly, He will make all things work for the good of those who remain faithful and love Him; this is His promise.[62]

Many parents who have suffered similar trials have utterly changed their lives as a result of their situation. Many have turned to God, learned how to be more selfless, turned away from bad habits and frivolous, sinful entertainment... Many parents in similar situations have turned to God with great zeal having better recognized how temporary earthly life is and how little control they have over it.

If this young child who has not reached the age of reason dies in right relationship with God through baptism and is welcomed into the glories of Heaven, then, that child has reached the very purpose for which he or she was created—to belong to God fully. The torment for the parents is inconceivable; however, what a lasting joy they will experience after this life if they grow in holiness through this trial and live their lives in accord with Christ's commands to the best of their abilities.

---

62   Romans 8:28: "We know that in everything God works for good with those who love him, who are called according to his purpose."

There is much good in reflecting on the joys of Heaven to the extent of properly realizing proportionately how fleeting are the woes of earthly life, including the profound woes that last until death. Perhaps God has allowed this young baptized child to suffer an early and unexpected death because He wants to use the prayers of this child in Heaven to pray for the marriage of his parents still living on earth, or for his sibling who is losing the faith, or for some other person or persons in need of help. All people belong to Him, the Creator of all things, the Author of all life. It is folly to accuse God of injustice when something occurs that is undesirable or seemingly beyond one's strength to endure. It is folly to allow pain to turn one away from God because only God grants the strength to endure and even embrace the pain well and even with peace.

God is good, trustworthy, omnipotent and omniscient. As hard as it might be, the strength to endure and even mature through periods of great turmoil is found by stubbornly holding fast to Him. The above-mentioned possibilities are ways to begin thinking more openly about God's power and perspective. They are not intended to be direct explanations for particular situations.

A false perspective of God and His actions in our lives can lead to depression, sinfulness, loss of faith, self-hatred, and much more. It is vital to look at the world in general, and suffering in particular, through the Catholic perspective. In doing so, even suffering and punishment is revealed as God's mercy. Because He is so powerful as to make good out of evil, there is no sin too great, no situation too disordered, no pain too acute for Him to make good out of it for those who remain faithful. They will grow in holiness, make reparations for more sins, reach a higher level of glory and perfection in Heaven, and merit grace for others as a result of God's generosity operating through deserved or undeserved suffering. Although further reflection on the points of Part 1 can offer much aid in accepting the suffering of this life, Part 2 will identify how God helps each faithful individual to bear his or her cross.

PART 2
Our Tools to Transform Suffering

In Part 2, we will explore the tools we have been given to transform suffering. We will start with examining the three theological virtues: faith, hope and charity. A virtue in general is a good habit. It can be understood as a muscle of the soul in that it must be exercised and put into practice in order for it to be more effective. Virtues are essential for spiritual growth, and through them a person is able to overcome temptation to lust, greed, wrath, envy.... The virtues of faith, hope, and charity in particular are called 'theological virtues' because their primary object is God. They differ from the other virtues that only help one's relationship to God indirectly. For instance, the virtue of temperance has the right ordering of bodily goods as its object. So, it helps a person to use in a moderate and ordered way bodily goods like food, drink, and sex. Faith, hope, and charity directly orient and order the person to God in a supernatural way.

These three virtues work in conjunction with man's reason and free will in order to help him to know, serve, and love God as God desires. As noted above, man is incapable of loving Him and even knowing Him as he ought; therefore, God offers various gifts which help man to overcome the many effects of sin that make it impossible to accept and live by the truths revealed in Sacred Scripture. Only with God's aid is it possible to fulfill Christ's words and follow closely His footsteps. Faith, hope, and charity are essential and most valuable components of God's aid. They are originally infused into the soul at baptism and strengthened as the Christian cooperates with God's grace, especially in the sacraments, but also in daily decisions. They are essential for salvation and ought to be understood and implemented in the life of every Christian. Each of these three virtues are radically helpful in our quests to suffer well.

CHAPTER 8

The Theological Virtue of Faith

"To one who has faith, no explanation is necessary. To one without faith, no explanation is possible."
—St. Thomas Aquinas

F aith is the virtue which helps the soul to assent to the revealed truths of Sacred Scripture. Any person who has done much to help an atheist see the logic and beauty of the Scriptures to no avail probably understands this point clearly. Because it is a gift, it cannot be earned or purchased by hours of study or a vast intelligence. Faith must be humbly received with an open heart. Therefore, the atheist will only receive and benefit from this gift by striving in honesty and humility to learn about God's existence and attributes.

However, faith helps in many more ways. It enables us to live by the truths we accept through faith. This virtue cannot be rightly understood as only belief. It is far more potent. Faith should form our very lives and draw us out of attachments to this life in order to begin living the life of Heaven now. Saint Francis Xavier observed: "It is not the actual physical exertion that counts towards one's progress, nor the nature of the task, but by the spirit of faith with which it is undertaken."[63] Faith fixates our views on God and the heavenly promised land.

In relation to suffering, faith is of significant value. Faith gives us a new vision to see God in and through all the happenings and events of earthly life. The Scriptures give evidence to this statement when Christ heals the two blind men because of their faith.[64] Similarly, when God gives faith to the open soul, He gives spiritual sight. Although this vision is vital, faith is only temporary. In this world where sin abounds, faith gives us a blurred vision of the spiritual world around us. Only in Heaven will a person be able to see God as He truly is, which is the fulfillment of all human desires (the Beatific Vision). Faith is the dimmed and imperfect view of God for the soul on the journey to Heaven, the one who has not yet arrived at his final destination. When practiced, it shapes our worldview and orders our steps on the narrow road.[65] It enables us to see beyond the veil of physical reality into the invisible reality all around.

For example, with the eyes of faith we recognize that the image of the man hanging on the cross is not some random criminal but the Son of God, Who suffered greatly in His human nature for the salvation of the world. By faith, the Christian recognizes in the Cross God's answer to his deepest questions and God's consolation to his deepest woes. All that was mentioned above concerning

---

63   Xavier, Saint Francis as quoted in *365 Days with the Saints*. Kelly-Gangi, Carol. Book Sales, 2015. p.254.
64   Matthew 9:27-29.
65   Matthew 7:14: "For the gate is narrow and the way is hard, that leads to life, and those who find it are few."

the importance and centrality of the Cross is only comprehended by way of faith.

Moreover, the eyes of faith see or at least recognize the presence of the underlying work of God's hands in daily occurrences. The eyes of faith see in the rising of the sun a reminder of the Resurrection of Jesus which dispersed the darkness of everlasting damnation for the faithful. The eyes of faith see sleep at night as a reminder of death and an encouragement to live rightly. The eyes of faith see that suffering is not an end nor an enemy. Rather, it is something that offers value to one's spiritual journey for the several reasons enumerated previously. The one with faith recognizes that God has a design that is far more valuable than one's own.

When suffering is without reason, without benefit, without remedy, it is too much to bear. Faith prevents us from listening to the thoughts and emotions that tend toward that false perception. The eyes of faith see that death is not a shut door, but for the faithful Christian it is the long-awaited and opened door to eternal reward. Because faith is a virtue, it is more or less effective for the soul according to the way it is implemented. Unfortunately, faith in the soul of many Christians is like a dusty book on the shelf, i.e. unused and unappreciated. If we practice faith daily, strive to live it in communion with and imitation of Christ, and make acts of faith regularly, then our dimmed vision of God's designs becomes clearer. We see the fingerprint of God in creation, in our neighbors, and especially in suffering. With greater faith, the soul can endure more sorrow, embrace more suffering, and do more good. In the throes of turmoil, we ought to be grateful for this gift and view our anguish and situations with it. Emotional, physical, mental, or spiritual pain is like a violent storm uprooting most people's interior peace. Faith in Christ calms the storm.[66] It does not deaden the pain, but it holds firmly to the One Who is known as the Prince of Peace.

Additionally, because faith helps the soul accept the truths of Sacred Scripture, it helps us to know God is loving and good regardless. Fear, confusion, and physical or emotional or mental anguish can paralyze us.[67] Faith releases the paralytic from his prison because he sees the loving and good God present to him in the suffering. It is medicine to the infected wound, breath to the empty lung, a parent to the lost and terrified child. For the one with great faith, God is ready to act.[68] Yet, faith is even more valuable when coupled with hope.

---

66   Mark 4:40: "Peace! Be still!" And the wind ceased, and there was a great calm. He said to them, "Why are you afraid? Have you no faith?"
67   Matthew 9:2: "And behold, they brought to him a paralytic, lying on his bed; and when Jesus saw their faith he said to the paralytic, "Take heart, my son; your sins are forgiven."
68   Matthew 21:23: "And whatever you ask in prayer, you will receive, if you have faith."

CHAPTER 9

The Theological
Virtue of Hope

"Pray, hope, and don't worry."
—*St. Padre Pio*

T he virtue of hope gives a powerful confidence in God, allowing a person to await the heavenly glory promised to those who remain faithful. It is very related to trust in God, Whose power and good will aims for the good of humanity. The Psalmist prays:

> "He who dwells in the shelter of the Most High, who abides in the shadow of the Almighty, will say to the Lord, 'My refuge and my fortress; my God, in whom I trust.' For he will deliver you from the snare of the fowler and from the deadly pestilence; he will cover you with his pinions, and under his wings you will find refuge; his faithfulness is a shield and buckler. You will not fear the terror of the night, nor the arrow that flies by day, nor the pestilence that stalks in darkness, nor the destruction that wastes at noonday. A thousand may fall at your side, ten thousand at your right hand; but it will not come near you. You will only look with your eyes and see the

recompense of the wicked. Because you have made the Lord your refuge, the Most High your habitation, no evil shall befall you, no scourge come near your tent. For he will give his angels charge of you to guard you in all your ways. On their hands they will bear you up, lest you dash your foot against a stone. You will tread on the lion and the adder, the young lion and the serpent you will trample under foot."[69]

This virtue is rather effective in times of great trial because it keeps the soul stalwart against surrendering to difficulty. Anybody who has experienced great turmoil understands the thoughts that begin to creep in suggesting that there is no way out, no solution.... Hope crushes these falsities, relentlessly resisting anything that denies the power and ability of God to aid and save His faithful children from any situation. It is a very powerful virtue in that there is no darkness or difficulty too much for the person who relentlessly holds firm to a well-developed virtue of hope.

Like faith, hope gives a supernatural sight. It allows the soul to see beyond the present suffering in order to persevere through it by a steady and unwavering confidence in the goodness of God. That is to say, by hope we see past the darkness of the crucifixion to the light of the Resurrection. The Book of Psalms reads, " I cry to thee, O Lord; I say, Thou art my refuge [hope], my portion in the land of the living."[70] Although we might feel helpless, exhausted, and defeated, hope stubbornly holds fast against a worsening situation because it illuminates the solution that is promised to come by God.

---

69   Psalms 91:1-13.

70   Psalms 142:5 (bracketed words added for clarification)

Multiple verses of Sacred Scripture speak of victory for those who love and serve Christ. Although many periods of strife dampen or make very distant that promise, hope reveals it with greater clarity. It sets our visions upon that promise and the perfect joy that will accompany it. Because hope gives the ability to await the good, it is invaluable in the long-lasting struggles of life. Think of the child who is left a paraplegic from a tragic accident. Think of the mother who loses her adolescent child to a terminal illness. Think of the man who killed an entire family while drunk driving. These and many other situations are painful to consider; however, hope is the firm foundation that prevents the darkness, the emotional turmoil, the unwanted thoughts, the fear of the future, and the ever-present sensation of loss from suffocating their victim by relentless attacks.

Saint Paul says, "Since we have such a hope, we are very bold."[71] It does not eradicate these turbulent circumstances, it enables one to advance despite them. Too often this virtue is misunderstood because of the lack of clarity in the English language. A child 'hopes spaghetti is for dinner' is an utterly different concept than the Christian who hopes in the mercy of God. The virtue of hope is powerful and effective, not passive nor baseless. God is the foundation for which we ought to have great hope. Because He is loving, good, generous, all-powerful, and compassionate, we ought to trust firmly and hope relentlessly in Him.

There is an alleged story where a woman, downtrodden and excessively woeful, approached St. Padre Pio about her deceased husband. St. Pio had the ability to read souls, which is a rare gift given for the conversion and edification of others, and at times

---

71   2 Corinthians 3:12.

he'd receive supernatural knowledge of events. In this particular story, the woman's husband had recently thrown himself from a cliff in an act of suicide. She was understandably distraught, but especially because it is a mortal sin to commit suicide. It is an act of rejection of God's mercy, God's Will, and the precious gift of life. She assumed his everlasting damnation because no one can enter Heaven or even Purgatory with a single intentionally committed and unconfessed mortal sin on their soul at the time of death.[72] Padre Pio, inspired by the grace of the Holy Spirit, informed her that her spouse confessed sincerely in an act of perfect contrition during his descent.

It is true that suicide is a mortal sin that does lead to hell; this is too often disregarded nowadays. It is also true that God is just and merciful and knows the hearts, minds, and circumstances of everyone. Thus, a person with grave mental difficulties who commits suicide acts without full knowledge and full freedom; he would not be fully culpable for the gravity of the sin. Therefore, even in the worst possible situations, one must always hope in the love and mercy of God.[73] To lose hope in Him is to lose confidence in Him. What child with a good and loving father loses confidence?

In one of the many letters St. Madeleine Sophie Barat received from Joseph-Marie Favre, her friend and spiritual guide, she read:

---

72   "But since all mortal sins, even those of thought, make men children of wrath (Eph 2:3) and enemies of God, it is necessary to ask pardon for all of them from God by an open and humble confession. While, therefore, the faithful of Christ strive to confess all sins which occur to their memory, they undoubtedly lay all of them before the divine mercy to be forgiven [can. 7]. While those who do otherwise and knowingly conceal certain sins, lay nothing before the divine bounty for forgiveness by the priest." (Denzinger-Hünermann 1680-1681.1682. Council of Trent, Session XIV, October 11, Confession, Ch. 5, 1551)

73   2 Corinthians 1:7: "Our hope for you is unshaken; for we know that as you share in our sufferings, you will also share in our comfort."

"Trust and the love of God gladden the heart, uplift the soul and make it capable of the greatest undertaking, whereas fear and mistrust depress and sadden the soul, shrink the heart, dull the spirit, ruin the health of the body.... How can you mistrust a God who infinitely loves you, who wishes only for your health and happiness? How you mistrust your dear, kind brother Jesus who has suffered so much to save you...."[74] We must fight against the temptations against hope, because it is a virtue given to us by God to help endure every trial and torment without surrender.

Like faith, hope is a virtue given only during the journey towards Heaven. It is the virtue that helps one persevere while waiting for Heaven. Therefore, once Heaven is achieved, it is no longer of value. However, in this life, hope can be lost by committing sins against it. This would include sins of despair. Even when a person falls into mortal sin, unless the sin is gravely and directly against faith or hope, these two virtues remain in the soul. God generously allows this so the soul might return to Him. When one is in dire need of Confession, hope is still available. When a person is in the state of sin, faith and hope are but shadows of what they are when they are accompanied by grace. Nevertheless, even in this incomplete state, they are still useful and significant for reversion. Hope is developed within the soul by making acts of hope, by praying for it, and by reflecting on the goodness of God. The more one considers His ways, the more confidence one gains in Him. The more confidence one has in God, the easier it is to love Him.

---

74   Joseph-Marie Favre in a letter written August 25th, 1832 addressed to St. Madaleine Sophie Barat in Chambéry.

CHAPTER 10

The Theological Virtue of Charity

"It is by the path of love, which is charity, that God draws near to man, and man to God. But where charity is not found, God cannot dwell. If, then, we possess charity, we possess God, for "God is Charity."
—St. Albert the Great

C harity, also translated as love, is the greatest of these three Theological Virtues.[75] It is the image of God's very own love poured into the human soul. This virtue is invaluable for several reasons and is also essential for salvation. Humanity is incapable of loving God in a dignified and worthy manner; He deserves to be loved in a far greater way. In order to have a proper and salvific relationship with God, something better than natural human love is needed. Images of natural human love include the love of a mother to her child, the love between friends, and the love of a man to his spouse. As good as these images are, God deserves far greater. Because man is not able to provide this to God, God gives this

---

75   1 Corinthians 13:13: "So faith, hope, love abide, these three; but the greatest of these is love."

supernatural love to the baptized in order that they might give it back to Him and to others. Charity enables us to love God above all things and all others. It is pure in that this supernatural love is for God's sake. That is, we love God for Who He is rather than what He can do for us. It binds our souls to Him and draws us toward God in greater ways. Charity attracts us away from the world and the temporary pleasures it can offer, toward the Creator. A soul steeped in Divine charity is a soul which lives for God alone. Through this supernatural love, our souls can give more, do more and even suffer more because God's strength resides within us.

This unique virtue accompanies grace given through the sacraments, which is a grace that dwells in the soul. It stays with us. Consequently, Divine charity is lost when this grace is lost, which occurs by committing a mortal sin. The life of the soul is the grace of God dwelling within it. Without this kind of grace and without the virtue of charity, the soul is separated from God, is spiritually lifeless and is incapable of doing anything that earns reward in Heaven. Saint Paul famously wrote,

> "If I speak in the tongues of men and of angels, but have not love, I am a noisy gong or a clanging cymbal. And if I have prophetic powers, and understand all mysteries and all knowledge, and if I have all faith, so as to remove mountains, but have not love, I am nothing. If I give away all I have, and if I deliver my body to be burned, but have not love, I gain nothing."[76]

Therefore, all of the suffering endured outside this state of grace is endured without the benefit of helping others spiritually,

---

76   1 Corinthians 13:1-3.

remitting temporal punishment, pleasing God, or becoming more Christ-like.[77]

Divine charity is precisely the mechanism which converts suffering into something of great value. In fact, the greater the love for God in one's sufferings, good works, spiritual practices..., the more pleasing they are to God and the more valuable they are to the soul. Saint Madeleine Sophie Barat taught, "Love our Lord deeply, love to imitate his spirit of sacrifice; can you wish for nothing but roses when you contemplate His Heart encircled with thorns? When He truly loves a soul, He keeps for it a place at the foot of the Cross [suffering] as He did for His Blessed Mother..."[78] Charity is this supernatural gift from God that empowers all that is done through it. Even the smallest gestures of mortification or acts of humility or faith or hope performed with great love are precious in the eyes of God and are exceptionally meritorious. This virtue inflames ordinary actions with the extraordinary love of God. The letter to the Colossians reads, "And above all these put on love, which binds everything together in perfect harmony."[79] God is love; therefore, the image of God's love poured into the Christian soul is the very essence of Christianity.

Moreover, charity enables us to love others for God's sake. To love God above all things and all others is to desire and love what and whom He desires and loves. Because God desires the salvation of all, we should desire, pray for, and pursue the salvation

---

77   Galatians 5:6: "For in Christ Jesus neither circumcision nor uncircumcision is of any avail, but faith working through love."

78   Barat, Saint Madeleine Sophie. Life of Blessed Madeleine Sophie Barat: Foundress of the Society of the Sacred Heart, 1779-1865. Roehampton [England] Publisher, 1908. p.115.

79   Colossians 3:14.

of others. The heart of Christ's command to "love your enemies and pray for those who persecute you"[80] is related to this idea. We must not only love in a natural way, which occurs through instinct and choice concerning those who seem lovable; we must love all people, including those who seem unlovable in their qualities, decisions, and character, with the supernatural love of God. He loves them; therefore, we do. God desires their conversion and salvation; therefore, we do. Christ manifests this love on the Cross in multiple ways, but very evidently as He cries, "Father, forgive them for they know not what they do."[81] In this light, Divine charity is extremely valuable in the midst of sorrow and suffering. This is the virtue that gives to suffering a meaning and a purpose. Truly, this truth is one of the most precious of the truths of the Catholic Church. The aging person of ninety years who is in a nursing home is far from useless, as society might suggest. That person is capable of offering countless rosaries and prayers and all his or her sufferings through great charity for the sake of the Church, the sanctity of the priests, the conversion of Muslims, the souls in Purgatory, etc. The boy bed-ridden with an incurable ailment may not be able to do house chores, help his parents pay the bills, or be an altar server, but he can save souls and live a heroic example of love by the way he suffers and prays with the virtue of charity. The mother of the mentally-challenged child may never have physical grandchildren, but by accepting this difficult task of care-taking for decades, day in and day out, with the virtue of Divine charity, she is able to bless countless people, grow in holiness, and participate in the salvation of numerous souls. Through this, she becomes a spiritual mother and grandmother to many in Heaven. The per-

---

80   Matthew 5:44.

81   Luke 23:34.

son with great charity is able to do more in small things to help his neighbor and his enemy than somebody else is able to do in great and difficult deeds done with little love.

The man who has never 'fit in' with others and has never had a good friend is far from alone if he possesses this supernatural love. This love binds the soul to Christ, but also to those bound to Him. It provides unity with God and community with all united to God. Therefore, this man is not only able to offer his sufferings of loneliness to the Father, through the sufferings of Christ, for other people who are lonely, he is also able to be consoled in the reality of the legion of saints and angels in Heaven who genuinely love and pray for him, the vast number of souls in Purgatory who count on him, and every person on earth in the state of grace who are in the trenches of spiritual warfare with him. What wondrous treasures of truth God has given to His Church. What magnificent virtues He uses to beautify the souls of His children.

Finally, charity conforms us to Christ. This virtue is increased by God's work in the soul. The Holy Spirit continues to offer graces which reveal opportunities to put into practice faith, hope, and love. These nudges of grace that direct the soul to do good and avoid evil are vital to the development of them. As the Christian implements these virtues in his daily decisions and general outlook, the Holy Spirit molds his soul into an image of the Savior. Through acts of faith, hope, and love, the Divine Artist purges the imperfections and wounds of sin and renovates the heart and mind with sublime splendor. Continue to develop them through prayer and practice, because as they increase, so do our endurance and resilience to suffering and resemblance to Jesus Christ.

In the time of suffering, the tendency is to focus on loss or abandonment. To remember and appreciate the three theological virtues in the midst of grief is to recognize the gifts of the loving Father that steady the waters of the raging storm. The Christian who understands and puts these into practice, particularly in periods of sorrow, is like the man alone in the ocean who suddenly comes across a life boat with water and food. It is so healing and uplifting to realize that God has given long ago all that is needed to embrace our crosses and to spiritually benefit from it. The three theological virtues directly relate to what was discussed in Part 1, because only with the eyes of faith, the eyes of hope, and the presence of Divine charity, can one begin to properly perceive suffering. Saint John of Avila wrote,

> "Dear brothers and sisters, I pray God may open your eyes and let you see what hidden treasures he bestows on us in the trials from which the world thinks only to flee. Shame turns into honor when we seek God's glory. Present affliction becomes the source of heavenly glory. To those who suffer wounds in fighting his battles God opens his arms in loving, tender friendship. That is why he (Christ) tells us that if we want to join him, we shall travel the way he took. It is surely not right that the Son of God should go his way on the path of shame while the sons of men walk the way of worldly honor: 'The disciple is not above his teacher, nor the servant greater than his master.'"[82]

Our goal is to change our perspectives — to look at every pain as a reminder to thank God that His mercy in this moment holds back the flames of hell. We must see every annoyance from

---

82   A letter written by Saint John of Avila.

spouses, parents, children, siblings, coworkers, or neighbors as an invitation from God to grow in the virtues of patience and meekness. We must see every woe as a thorn from Christ's crown to be cherished, and every unwanted thought as a spiritual vitamin for the building of virtue. Through faith, hope, and charity, thoughts of lust are changed to the virtue of chastity, resentment to forgiveness, judgment to kindness, blasphemy to religion, past memories of sins or embarrassment to purity, vanity to humility, hatred to meekness, etc. There is no arrow of the enemy, no attack of the devil, that faith, hope, and charity cannot transform into something of benefit. These virtues in conjunction with the graces God offers in times of distress are more than sufficient to carry forward the Christian who does not impede His help. Through faith, hope, and charity, we have all the proof necessary to know and experience God as the loving Father He is, even in the darkest valleys of human experience.

CHAPTER 11

The Sacrament of Confession

"Confession heals, confession justifies, confession grants pardon of sin, all hope consists in confession; in confession there is a chance for mercy."
-St. Isidore of Seville

The seven Sacraments of the Catholic Church are very relevant to human suffering in that they are seven fountains of grace and mercy showered on the soul for the purpose of salvation and sanctification. The *Catechism* explains, "The sacraments are efficacious signs of grace, instituted by Christ and entrusted to the Church, by which divine life is dispensed to us."[83] Jesus Christ personally gave each of the seven sacraments to the apostles to build up the Church by making souls holy. To be holy is to be 'set apart' by God and for God. This is possible only through intimate union with Christ. Therefore, the seven sacraments offer this intimate union. Although each of them serve a different purpose and give a special grace, they all enrich the soul with sanctifying grace which

---

83   Catholic Church, *Catechism of the Catholic Church*, 2nd Ed. (Washington, DC: United States Catholic Conference, 2000), 293.

strengthens unity with God and increases faith, hope, and charity in the soul. Each of the sacraments can be understood to have a positive effect with regard to suffering; however, the Sacrament of Reconciliation and the Sacrament of the Most Holy Eucharist are most pertinent to this book. Both of them offer assistance to the sufferer which cannot be found elsewhere. In addition, both of these sacraments teach an attribute of the Christian way of life that is directly related to our capacity to carry crosses.

Without question, the Sacrament of Reconciliation, also known as penance or confession, is one of the most precious gifts God has given to humanity. When we have great guilt and remorse, few words are as valuable to hear as a priest saying, "I absolve you from your sins in the name of the Father and of the Son and of the Holy Spirit." In this sacrament, Christ (the Good Shepherd) finds his lost sheep and returns him or her to the flock. In this sacrament, Christ satisfies His 'thirst' for souls which He declares from the Cross.[84] We walk into the confessional riddled with sin and guilt and walk right back out without the blemish of sin remaining. Though many people think it's terrifying (or terrible) to confess sins to another human person, this is an impoverished view of community, Church, hierarchy, authority, and Christianity. G. K. Chesterton once said, "The morbid thing is NOT to confess [your sins]. The morbid thing is to conceal your sins and let them eat away at your soul, which is exactly the state of most people in today's highly civilized communities"[85] He also clarified the purpose of the Sacrament of Penance:

---

84   John 19:28: "After this Jesus, knowing that all was now finished, said (to fulfil the scripture), 'I thirst.'"

85   G.K. Chesterton as quoted in Ahlquist, Dale. *The Complete Thinker: The Marvelous Mind of G.K. Chesterton.* Ignatius Press, San Francisco, 2012. p.69.

"The real difference between the Church and State is huge and plain. The State, in all lands and ages, has created a machinery of punishment, bloodier and more brutal in some places than in others, but bloody and brutal everywhere. The Church is the only institution that ever attempted to create a machinery of pardon. The Church is the only thing that ever attempted by system to pursue and discover crimes, not in order to avenge, but in order to forgive them..."[86]

The only critique to this statement is that Christ instituted this 'machinery of pardon;' the Church simply organizes and implements it. Regardless, Chesterton demonstrates how the Sacrament of Penance is directly connected to the Church's Mission on earth–– to glorify God and to save souls.

Lest anyone think this is irrelevant to suffering, the connection between sin and suffering ought to be well-established. Sin disorders humanity. These disorders invariably end with suffering of some sort or another. Therefore, any sacrament that puts back into order the soul of a sinner is a sacrament that prevents the increase of suffering and begins to heal the soul. Christ said,

"Tell souls where they are to look for solace; that is, in the Tribunal of Mercy [the confessional]. There the greatest miracles take place [and] are incessantly repeated. To avail oneself of this miracle, it is not necessary to go on a great pilgrimage or to carry out some external ceremony; it suffices to come with faith to the feet of My representative and to reveal to him one's misery, and the miracle of Divine Mercy will be fully demonstrated. Were a soul like a decaying corpse so that from a human standpoint, there would be no [hope of] resto-

---

86   Chesterton, G.K. *Complete Works of G.K. Chesterton*. Deplphi Classics, 2013.

ration and everything would already be lost, it is not so with God. The miracle of Divine Mercy restores that soul in full. Oh, how miserable are those who do not take advantage of the miracle of God's mercy! You will call out in vain, but it will be too late."[87]

Consolation of the soul, peace of mind, and the mercy of God are found in the confessional.

Certainly, the Sacrament of Penance is related to sorrow. It does not matter what kind of sorrow is experienced or the cause of it, Confession is instrumental. Although the emotion or sensation of peace is given somewhat regularly, this is an extra grace from God which is not the focus nor the purpose of the sacrament. Draw near to the merciful One Who cleans the soul, restores supernatural life, and strengthens resolve to overcome future temptation.

Confession is More Than the Forgiveness of Sins

Confession is not just the forgiveness of sins. If it were nothing more, it would be entirely worth it; however, God is more generous. Many graces flow through it for the benefit of the penitent [the one who confesses]. Reconciliation is to the soul what a shower is to the body. The body needs to be cleaned to smell better — this helps in keeping friends. Cleansing gets rid of germs, which fends off infection and prevents some diseases from spreading to another person.

A shower refreshes us, especially when it is a much-needed one. The Sacrament of Confession is similar because it cleanses

---

87   Saint Faustina. *Divine Mercy in My Soul.* Marian Press, Stockbridge, 2003. 1448.

our souls from sin (as already stated), but it also begins the healing process of the wounds caused by those sins. Moreover, the penance given by the priest pays some temporal punishment and pledges to God a hope to avoid sin. As these sins are cleansed and some of the effects of sin removed, we more easily affect others only for the good. That is to say that sins (and their effects) lingering in our souls do more and more harm to us and those with whom we communicate. When we leave the confessional, we are refreshed by the graces received and renewed by Christ's mercy. We are granted more strength to overcome those sins as the temptations rise in the future.

Finally, reconciliation is a precursor to the Eucharist. Through it, we are better disposed to receive worthily and well the Body and Blood of the Savior. Like the bride who is meticulous in her preparations to encounter her beloved at the altar for holy matrimony, so we should be careful in how we prepare our souls to encounter Christ, the Bridegroom, at the altar. All this and more because God is truly merciful. This forgiveness is truly valuable to the person who suffers. Especially those who suffer from self-abasement, self-hatred, and poor self-esteem can find in this sacrament the ability to forgive one's self.

A common source of strife is discontentment with self. So many believe that self-worth is based on their looks, habits, finances, career, intelligence, athletic ability, their spouse, or their popularity, etc. These are lies from the pit of hell. The worth of a human person is founded upon the dignity which he or she has received from our Creator. For those who are baptized, that worth is also based on the relationship we have as a child of God. The confessional is where Christ reveals this worth to us. No matter our positions in life, successes, popularities, colors, races, ages, weights, or genders, sins are remitted when they are contritely confessed well. Regardless of the size or the quantity of the sins, God's mercy is larger. Therefore, in this situation we are healed of many wounds and slowly leave behind our suffering by learning to forgive ourselves. Confession helps us to recognize our true value by seeing ourselves through God's eyes rather than the eyes of another or our own deficient self-perceptions. The diabolic lies which suggest, "I am not worthy or worth it," "God would not forgive me," "I am too damaged to save..." are all shattered by the universal call from Christ to accept His mercy. The confessional teaches us that our past failures or present condition do not change God's desire for our salvation. God desires the good for man. "And God saw everything that he had made, and behold, it was very good."[88] Although sin certainly affects this original state of goodness in which man was created, it does not deter God from seeing what the penitent could be if he would just trustingly open himself to His light. As death had no hold over Jesus, so sin has no power over the Sacrament of Penance.

People are slow to confess because they do not always know what to say; or, they get tired of saying the same thing every time; or, because they are embarrassed. These are simply temptations; God does not grow tired of forgiving the contrite sinner; the sinner should not grow tired of begging for mercy.[89] The priest is there simply to help in the process, not to judge or match sins with sinners in the future. The saints frequented the confessional. Some of them confessed every day. Many encouraged people to use this

---

88   Genesis 1:31.

89   Luke 15:7: "Just so, I tell you, there will be more joy in heaven over one sinner who repents than over ninety-nine righteous persons who need no repentance."

sacrament at least once per week. If the holiest confessed often, should not the rest of humanity?

The Sacrament of Penance becomes a model to alleviate many torments. As we often experience the limitless mercy of God in the confessional, we are encouraged to be more forgiving of others. Forgiveness is an extremely useful habit to develop for the sake of spiritual, mental, and emotional health. Christ says, "For if you forgive men their trespasses, your heavenly Father also will forgive you; but if you do not forgive men their trespasses, neither will your Father forgive your trespasses."[90] To withhold forgiveness is to harm one's self instead of the other. There is no gain in it. It keeps wounds of the soul open and causes infection and terrible consequences. Unforgiveness destroys marriages and families, ruins lives, and can even lead to physical problems and suicide. Saint Paul gives the formula of spiritual health as he also emphasizes forgiveness: "Put on then, as God's chosen ones, holy and beloved, compassion, kindness, lowliness, meekness and patience, forbearing one another and, if one has a complaint against another, forgiving each other; as the Lord has forgiven you, so you also must forgive."[91] By forgiving, the soul imitates the love of God and releases some internal disorder, disinfecting the wound and allowing the healing process to begin.

Unfortunately, forgiveness is often misunderstood. Many people seem to think that forgiveness means to be able to forget something. This is nonsense because forgetfulness is involuntary. There are things we want to remember which we forget, and we forget things we wish to remember. God does not command something

---

90   Matthew 6:15.
91   Colossians 3:12-13.

that is involuntary. He gave free will in order for us to choose to fulfill His commands through love. Forgiveness is a choice, an act of the will. Therefore, it is possible to forgive a person, but to remember and despise what they've done. In fact, it is even possible to forgive a person while still feeling emotionally hurt from the offense.

Additionally, it is common for a person to have to forgive somebody for the same offense multiple times. The deeper the wound, the more likely it will be reopened when some event or some situation prods it. This is not a problem; rather, it is simply another opportunity to be more like Christ and forgive the person again.[92] If one develops the habit of controlling his or her thoughts, forgiveness is much easier. Not dwelling on some word or deed a person enacted is half the battle. Praying for the person is a good indication that we have forgiven them or are in the process of doing so. As the spiritual life matures, these words make more sense: "But I say to you, love your enemies and pray for those who persecute you."[93] Again, "Blessed are you when men revile you and persecute you and utter all kinds of evil against you falsely on my account. Rejoice and be glad, for your reward is great in heaven, for so men persecuted the prophets who were before you."[94] When we are able to forgive easily, we have a great resilience to suffering and sorrow because we so quickly move past these wounds and insults. Forgiveness is a power over the enemy who seeks to use the wounds of the soul as a pressure point to induce strife, sin, and

---

92   Luke 17:3-4: "Take heed to yourselves; if your brother sins, rebuke him, and if he repents, forgive him; and if he sins against you seven times in the day, and turns to you seven times, and says, 'I repent,' you must forgive him."

93   Matthew 5:44.

94   Matthew 5:11-12.

despair. Perhaps a reason Christ never tires of forgiving those who are contrite and desirous to live a better life is that He patiently and repeatedly shows the importance of acquiring this habit.

Finally, we must also learn to forgive ourselves, to view ourselves through God's perspective: One who is made in His Image. He loves us immensely. We should trust in that love and learn to view ourselves through it. If God finds us worthy of forgiveness, who are we to refuse to pardon ourselves? This task can prove to be most difficult for some people. Resentment and hatred toward self begins to develop. These wounds amplify terrible thoughts and cause incalculable damage to several relationships. Forgiveness is our freedom from this torment, a source of healing for the soul, and a means to follow more closely the footsteps of Christ.

Jesus spends three years of His earthly life healing the blind, paralyzed, deaf, possessed, and many others. Through these miracles He demonstrates His tender Mercy and intense desire to heal. By inviting Christ into past memories of sin, embarrassment, and pain, He begins to restore even the deepest wounds that affect every aspect of life. Through prayer, forgiveness, and especially the Sacrament of Reconciliation, the Divine Physician refreshes and renews proper order and health to His disciples.

CHAPTER 12

The Body, Blood, Soul, and Divinity of Jesus

"The devotion to the Eucharist is the most noble, because it has God as its object; it is the most profitable for salvation, because it gives us the Author of Grace; it is the sweetest, because the Lord is Sweetness Itself."
—*St. Pope Pius X*

Another sacrament that has a direct impact on how well a person suffers is the Most Holy Eucharist. It is the summit of the Christian faith and the center of the Catholic's life. It is the high point of the Holy Sacrifice of the Mass, which is the universal prayer of the Church and the ultimate form of public worship. The Eucharist is the pinnacle of union with God in this life. The Body, Blood, Soul, and Divinity of Jesus Christ is given for human consumption in an inexpressible act of generosity and mercy. In short, the Mass is a perfect prayer because it allows all those united to Christ through grace to participate in His perfect sacrifice on the Cross.

The sacrifice of Christ is the fulfillment of the four kinds of sacrifice of the Old Testament:

1. *Adoration* is given by Christ on the Cross because the highest form of adoration is sacrifice. The highest form of sacrifice is the sacrifice of the perfect, unblemished, and sacred Lamb of God. He gives Himself to the Father in loving adoration by enduring all the anguish of the Passion in loving submission to His Will.

2. *Reparation* is obviously inherent in the death of Jesus. His death is so valuable and precious that it is sufficient to forgive every sin ever committed. No other act of reparation can remotely rival its worth. What all the sacrificed lambs of the Old Testament could not supply (a worthy sacrifice), is provided on Calvary.

3. *Supplication* is the most popular form of prayer; yet, only on the Cross does it find its consummate form. Jesus Christ offers Himself on behalf of humanity to heal, sanctify, and save all who submit to Him. Through His merits, the answers to prayers are given. Without Christ's death, there is no relationship between God and man. Because His life and death reestablish this relationship, He gives meaning to the petitions of man. Through His death, man calls God 'Father,' Savior,' and 'Lord.' Every Christian's supplication in prayer is connected to the Cross. Christ's gift of Himself to the Father is the perfect petition for the salvation of humanity.

4. *Thanksgiving* offered to God is brought to its pinnacle in the death of Jesus Christ. How can man give adequate thanksgiving to the Father Who gave His own Son for lowly creatures? The answer is humble, grateful, and loving participation in the sacrifice of His Son. That is to say, when the faithful reverently and devoutly receive the Eucharist, they proclaim and profess

the mercy of God, the importance of the Cross, and the magnanimity of God. When a father gives his child a present, it is a form of gratitude for the child to responsibly use and enjoy it. The Christian expresses profound gratitude by availing himself to this sacrament after sincere preparation of mind and heart. Saint John Vianney noticed, "Nothing afflicts the heart of Jesus so much as to see all His sufferings of no avail to so many."[95]

The Lord suffers in vain for those who do not accept the fruit produced from the tree upon which He died. Through humble participation in the Mass and reverent, devout reception of the Eucharist, God is pleased. He desires to save humanity so much as to give Himself for it; how delighted He is when humanity does not abuse or reject His gift. Separated from the Cross, no man can offer God adequate sacrifice, but united to it, the Father sees the small gift of the faithful united to the most dignified gift of His Son. Therefore, in the Eucharist the faithful have the opportunity to give perfect thanksgiving to God. Individually our thanksgiving is not perfect because of our sins and imperfections, but when our gratitude is united to Christ's sacrifice, it is made perfect through Him. The word 'Eucharist' is derived from the word 'εὐχαριστία' meaning 'thanksgiving.' Every time we receive Holy Communion properly disposed, we uniquely please God. We express profound gratitude by availing ourselves to this sacrament after sincere preparation of mind and heart. The more we center our lives around the Eucharist, the more pleasing our Holy Communions are and the more efficacious they are for us.

---

95   -Saint John Vianney as quoted in Bowden, Edward. *The Spirit of the Cure D'Ars.* Salzwasser-Verlag, 2022. p.195.

Man has always been incapable of giving adequate adoration, adequate reparation, adequate supplication, adequate gratitude to a Being so superior and so sublime. However, the God-man is able to do so on behalf of all humanity. Therefore, whoever is united to Him and His sacrifice of perfect adoration, perfect reparation, perfect supplication, and perfect thanksgiving is able to give to God a most pleasing sacrifice indeed.

It is not possible for us to overestimate the importance of the Eucharist. Libraries have been filled with the benefits and teachings of It. Saint Maximilian Kolbe taught, "If angels could be jealous of men, they would be so for one reason: Holy Communion."[96] Saint John Vianney remarked, "There is nothing so great as the Eucharist. If God had something more precious, He would have given it to us."[97] The Eucharist is the visible, edible, and touchable sign that Christ wants nothing less for us than Himself. He wants to fill our souls, heal our wounds, and provide us with peace. Every time we approach Holy Communion, come as the sick to the doctor, the hungry to the feast, the lonely to a friend, the orphan to a mother, the poor to eternal riches. Offer Him every single pain, wound, and insecurity. Trustingly beg Him to take everything, heal everything, and bless us immensely. Still, so many people stay away not realizing this to be the source of peace for the journey to Heaven. It is a foretaste of Heaven and a treasure without measure.

The Eucharist is how we enter into the very sacrifice of Christ crucified. Everything already discussed concerning the Cross of Christ is made an intimate reality to us through the Eucharist. In

---

96   Saint Maximilian Kolbe. Tassone, Susan. *Jesus Speaks to Faustina and You.* Sophia Institute Press, Manchester, 2020. p.22.

97   Saint John Vianney. Onuoha, Chima Kelechi. *Towards a Deeper Understanding of the Holy Mass.* First Edition Design Publications, 2019.

receiving Holy Communion, we join Him on the Cross and we exit the tomb with our risen Lord.

Christ boldly taught, "For my flesh is food indeed, and my blood is drink indeed. He who eats my flesh and drinks my blood abides in me, and I in him. As the living Father sent me, and I live because of the Father, so he who eats me will live because of me. This is the bread which came down from heaven, not such as the fathers ate and died; he who eats this bread will live forever."[98] The Eucharist is a medicine for the soul by which God communicates His Divine Life to His children. It heals wounds caused by sin, division, and disharmony. These wounds are not healed by a first aid kit; rather, the help and grace from the Holy Spirit is the much-needed recipe for recovery. These wounds affect perception, cause ruptures in relationships, and amplify interior turbulence. How many divorces, broken homes, lost friendships, ended careers, etc. could be avoided if we would tend to the wounds of the soul? These wounds are caused by our own sins as well as the sins of others committed against us. Additionally, wounds can emerge from suffering.

The Eucharist is a Fountain of Healing

Praying daily to the Blessed Virgin and her spouse, the Holy Spirit, to heal us is very effective in restoring health. However, the Eucharist is also a fountain of healing for the soul. The more faith and charity with which we consume the Holy Eucharist, the more grace enters into our souls, the more malleable our hearts are in the hands of God, and the more effectively we overcome these wounds. Jesus is the Divine Physician providing to His patients

---

98   John 6:55-58.

both health and vitality. Sin deadens zeal for God, and it poisons peace. In opposition to this, the Eucharist is a taste of Eternal Life which unites us to the Prince of Peace.[99] This sacrament is not a magic trick or superstition, without the state of grace, faith, devotion, trust, persistence, or charity, It has no good effect.[100] Suffering can cause the soul to turn inwardly; the Eucharist draws open the door of the soul to the Author of Life. Suffering can cause resentment and hatred; the Eucharist is the Sacrament of Love and the taste of mercy.[101] Suffering can cause one to abandon God; the Eucharist is proof of the nearness of the Redeemer. Suffering can cause despair; the Eucharist is the pledge of everlasting glory. What water is to the thirsty, the Eucharist is to the weak and wounded. Whatever wounds we obtain in life are healed more and more by this sacrament which is given directly from God as the remedy for sin, suffering, and damnation. In His generosity, God made Himself, His love, and mercy edible by the consecrated Host which still appears to be bread and wine but are truly the Body, Blood, Soul, and Divinity of Jesus Christ.

Furthermore, the Body and Blood of Christ offer a spiritual strength necessary for the soul to reach the heights of sanctity which God desires for it. Food helps the body by providing the necessary strength to fight disease, function properly, grow, and work. The Eucharist does the same for the soul. Saint Ignatius

---

99   Saint Padre Pio: "Always remain close to the Catholic Church, because it alone can give you true peace, since it alone possesses Jesus in the Blessed Sacrament, the true Prince of Peace." as quoted in Evert, Jason. *Purity 365.* Totus Tuus Press.

100   1 Corinthians 11:29: "For anyone who eats and drinks without discerning the body eats and drinks judgment upon himself."

101   "In the sacrament of the Eucharist, Jesus shows us in particular the truth about the love which is the very essence of God." Pope Benedict XVI in *Sacramentum Caritatis.*

wrote, "One of the most admirable effects of Holy Communion is to preserve the soul from sin, and to help those who fall through weakness to rise again."[102] It provides the strength of Christ in some measure for the disciple to follow His Lord. With all the temptation and darkness, the Eucharist provides protection from the attacks of the enemy, the temptations of the world, and our own weaknesses. Christ explained to Saint Faustina, "I desire to unite Myself to human souls, Know, My daughter, that when I come to a human heart in Holy Communion, My hands are full of all kinds of graces which I want to give to the soul. But souls do not even pay any attention to Me; they leave Me to Myself and busy themselves with other things...They treat Me as a dead object."[103] He longs to help the suffering. Virtue is the necessary strength to fight off the disease of vice and wickedness; the Eucharist provides grace and virtue. Sin causes disorder within the soul; the Eucharist reestablishes that order while fortifying it from future afflictions. Suffering can stunt spiritual growth when not accepted properly; the Eucharist conforms the soul to the Savior, providing a spiritual maturity which enables us to fulfill God's Will and save souls through His grace.

The Eucharist empties our souls of self-love to make room for Christ to dwell and operate in us. As a cleanse purifies the body of toxins, the Eucharist purifies the soul of the relics of sin.[104] Saint Paul noted, "I have been crucified with Christ; it is no longer I who live, but Christ who lives in me; and the life I now live in

---

102   Saint Ignatius of Loyola as quoted in Burke, John James. *Mary, Help of Christians, and the Fourteen Saints Invoked as Joly Helpers.* Benzinger Brothers, 2007. p380.
103   Saint Faustina. *Divine Mercy in My Soul.* 1385.
104   Relics of sin are effects of sin that linger even once the sins have been forgiven. Temporary punishment and wounds are examples of these.

the flesh I live by faith in the Son of God, who loved me and gave himself for me."[105] If Catholics in periods of great torment would only recognize the invaluable source of healing and strength they have offered to them in the Sacrament of Love, they would not hesitate to receive from their spiritual fathers, the priests, this treasure of inestimable value. What the therapist and the doctor provide physically and emotionally (as helpful as it may be) pale in comparison to what the priest provides spiritually, mentally, emotionally, and physically through the distribution of Holy Communion. The Prince of Peace longs to give Himself to His followers, to each of us; we ought to let Him.

Resulting from the great wisdom of Holy Mother Church, Holy Communion is not the only way to derive benefit from the Body and Blood of Christ. Eucharistic exposition is a period of time in which the Eucharist is exposed in a monstrance (a vessel which holds the Eucharist in a way to allow it to be seen by the faithful) for the people to adore. This is a most beneficial practice. In fact, nearness to the Eucharist is valuable in any form. Even if the Eucharist is reserved in the tabernacle, there is much benefit to be in the church keeping Him company. Consistently it is discovered time and time again that whenever a person places himself before the Eucharist with some regularity, he or she finds peace. Every Catholic should find a refuge from the rush of daily life in the tabernacle. The soul who suffers from anxiety, depression, family problems, emotional turmoil, spiritual aridity, internal turbulence, mental chaos, loss, or any other difficulty should be regular in visiting the Most Blessed Sacrament. It is calm to the storm, silence to the noise, order to the chaos, harmony to the

---

105   Galatians 2:20.

discord, light to the darkness, and life to death. There are no words which can adequately explain the benefits of a Eucharistic devotion. Adoration of the Eucharist leads to peace of heart. The Little Flower understood, "Do you realize that Jesus is there in the tabernacle expressly for you – for you alone? He burns with the desire to come into your heart...don't listen to the demon, laugh at him, and go without fear to receive the Jesus of peace and love."[106]

By simply stopping for five minutes at the church on route to work or elsewhere, the peace of Christ will begin to calm the inescapable winds of suffering.[107] With just a little trust and consistency, no storm is too aggressive, too mighty, or too long to endure with Christ. Visiting the Eucharist in the tabernacle is like Christ waking in the boat to find His apostles fearful at the desperate situation. He awakes, rebukes the turbulence, and restores security and peace to His followers.[108] Have enough faith to seek out Christ in the Eucharist and all the necessary help, healing, and courage will be found. For parents, bring your children to these five-minute visits to the Blessed Sacrament in order to show them that our refuge is not in the distraction of entertainment or the false escape of drugs or alcohol, but in the tabernacle where Jesus waits for us. In doing so, they will learn well that their stronghold

---

106   Saint Thérèse of Lisieux as quoted in Brother Francis Mary, FI. *Saint Therese: Doctor of the Little Way.* Academy of the Immaculate, 1998. p.153.

107   If the church is locked, pray in the car or walk the grounds of the church while praying.

108   Mark 4:37-39: "And a great storm of wind arose, and the waves beat into the boat, so that the boat was already filling. But he was in the stern, asleep on the cushion; and they woke him and said to him, "Teacher, do you not care if we perish?" And he awoke and rebuked the wind, and said to the sea, "Peace! Be still!" And the wind ceased, and there was a great calm."

and peace are found in the nearest Catholic Church. This practice may be most important of everything they learn.

Gratitude and the Eucharist

Gratitude is one of the last things a person considers when enduring difficulties. Generally, thoughts of self-pity tend to overwhelm and tune out other kinds of thoughts, especially in relation to others. Admittedly, it is difficult to be grateful in these times. Nevertheless, gratitude continues to be a valuable shield which prevents suffering from turning to hatred, thoughts from becoming negative, and healing from being halted. When we are sincerely grateful for our lives and blessings from God, we are more capable of enduring and confronting trials and failures well. On the other hand, when we feel entitled to our possessions and desires, we are pierced more deeply by the sword of sorrow. Additionally, we are less equipped to embrace that turmoil and use it for personal and spiritual growth. When the wounds caused by suffering are left untreated, they become infected and cause many more trials and much more suffering. Gratitude helps prevent this occurrence by reflection on God's goodness, the help of others, and the recognition that we are undeserving. It opens our souls to look upward and outward toward God rather than inward toward self. Because the Eucharist is the perfect act of gratitude from the Son to the Father through the Holy Spirit, it is directly related to the faithful who are united to Christ by the reception of this sacrament. The Eucharist makes a grateful heart, and a grateful heart makes a joyful soul.

Too often the many goods and blessings of life are forgotten or ignored. This is especially true concerning the spiritual goods liberally given by God. The Eucharist is the best reminder of God's marvelous gifts because It is God Himself. Having consumed the Body of Christ, the Christian can encounter any battle or attack of that day with certainty of an increase in Christ's help. Therefore, reflection on the Eucharist breeds relentless gratitude. We all should develop the habit of giving thanks to God every day for the many benefits enjoyed by His benevolence. This prayer ought not be overly cumbersome but childlike and sincere. The more cumbersome a prayer, the less consistently it will be prayed. In a prayer of thanksgiving, we should begin with the greatest benefits which relate to spiritual blessings and then give consideration to others. Here is an example of a daily prayer of gratitude:

"God the Father, I give You thanks for Your creation, providence, holy Will and the life you give me. God the Son, I give You thanks for the Incarnation, Passion, death, and Resurrection which You endured for my salvation. I thank You for Your Most Precious Blood, Most Sacred Heart, and the grace and mercy You give. God the Holy Ghost, I thank you for indwelling in my soul, Your work of applying the merits of Christ to my soul, uniting me to Christ through the Church, and serving me as my Divine Friend Who leads me to holiness through love. Thank You Most Holy Trinity. Thank you for making the pure and Blessed Mother Mary my mother also. Thank You for the seven sacraments through which you conform me to Your Will. I am especially grateful for my baptism, my confirmation, Holy reconciliation and The Most Holy Eucharist [add another applicable sacraments e.g. holy matrimony...]. I am grateful for the guardian angel you offer me for my protection along with the help of Saint Michael, my patron, Saint Joseph, Saint Bonaventure, Saint John Vianney, Saint

Mary Magdalene, Saint Gemma Galgani, Saint Maria Goretti, Saint Pius X [namely, any saint with whom one has formed a relationship].... I give you thanks Almighty God for my life, my body, my family, friends, career, shelter, health and all other benefits. Lastly, I give thanks to you, holy mother, for your care and aid, to you, guardian angel, for your guidance, and to you, saints of Heaven, for your intercession. Amen."

Through the Most Holy Eucharist, God gives to humanity the universal medicine, the all-inclusive antidote. Through devotion to It, we will find the strength to harness any form of suffering as a weapon for the glory of God and the salvation of souls. The Eucharist is the model for suffering. The Eucharist is the suffering of Christ made salvific and available to humanity. The reception of Holy Communion plunges our souls into the boundless love of Christ. Therefore, we ought, by the graces which flow through this sacrament, to convert our woes into a precious gift to God for the salvation of others. The Eucharist is sacrificial self-gift, which binds our souls to our Savior. When we carry our crosses and offer them for the benefit of others, we resemble the gift of the Eucharist. We are Christ-like in that we offer ourselves for the benefit of another. Finally, through the Eucharist, we give worthy gratitude to the Father and develop a grateful heart, which is vital to embracing our crosses lovingly and stimulating peace for the soul.

CHAPTER 13

Armor for Sorrows

"The road is narrow. He who wishes to travel it more easily must cast off all things and use the cross as his cane. In other words, he must be truly resolved to suffer willingly for the love of God in all things."
—St. John of the Cross

T he Catholic way of life is filled with spiritual practices handed down by the holy men and women who reached the peak of sanctity. They are the teachers of holiness, the masters of the spiritual life. How beneficial it is to follow their examples. There are a few spiritual practices that can serve as an armor for the Christian who encounters suffering of various kinds. As armor is worn prior and throughout the battle, so these practices are to be implemented consistently so as to prepare us for whatever may come. They will serve as a protection against turmoil if they become habits. They will not prevent pain entirely, but they can serve to prevent its amplification and directly aid us in enduring and embracing it. These three practices are mortification, custody of the mind, and meditation.

First, mortification is a word derived from Latin meaning to 'make dead.' When we mortify, we deny ourselves the desires and pleasures of the flesh. We are willing to deny ourselves personal comforts, desires, or pleasures, for a greater purpose. Christ denied Himself when He fasted for forty days in the desert, taught truth (even against the common religious leaders of His day), and embraced the Cross despite the inexpressible torments that accompanied it.[109]

Mortification trains our souls to be detached from our own wills. If we are accustomed to always eating and drinking whatever and whenever we want, watching television as much as we want, and doing generally whatever we like, we become attached to our own wills. We are angered when something is contrary to our desires. We are sorrowful at the things we cannot control. We become enslaved to our own wants and find it difficult to accept disappointment. Mortification purifies our souls from this vulnerable and dangerous state. It empties us of disordered self-love so that greater love for God can fill the soul.

When we are slaves to our own desires, many problems and wounds are caused by the frustration of our wills. However, when we train ourselves in mortification, we are able to endure hardship, controversy, and disappointment well. Mortification is not limited to fasting. Anytime we are willing to deny our own desires for the sake of submitting to God's Will, we die to self.[110] The letter to the Romans explains, "For if you live according to the flesh you will die, but if by the Spirit you put to death the deeds of the body you will live."[111]

---

109   Matthew 4:1-4, Matthew 12, Luke 22-23.
110   Mark 8:34-35: "And he called to him the multitude with his disciples, and said to them, 'If any man would come after me, let him deny himself and take up his cross and follow me. For whoever would save his life will lose it; and whoever loses his life for my sake and the gospel's will save it.'"
111   Romans 8:13.

Too often, we fail to recognize the countless opportunities of mortification that present themselves throughout our days. For instance, if we desire to watch television we mortify ourselves by simply praying three Hail Marys before turning the television on. If we desire to turn the fan on for more comfort, we mortify ourselves by accepting the small discomfort that comes from the heat. If we desire to listen to music during work, we mortify ourselves by working in silence for an hour or the whole day. If we desire to sleep a little longer, we mortify ourselves by waking up five minutes earlier every day to spend a few extra minutes in prayer. If we desire to continue walking, we mortify ourselves to stop and pick up a piece of trash. *The key is that we do these things for love of God.* There is nothing inherently beneficial about picking up trash or waking up earlier, but when these tasks are accomplished for love of God and to mortify our own desires, they are remarkably beneficial in our spiritual lives. Choosing a few small and achievable mortifications each day builds this habit and layers our souls with a resilience to disappointment.

Mortification is a kind of armor or protection from suffering, not in that it prevents suffering; nothing in this book is meant to do so. Rather, as we grow accustomed to denying ourselves more and more, we are able to cope and handle disappointment and hardship with greater peace. When we are attached to our own wills we are more greatly tried by the unexpected. Mortification is valuable for several reasons, as so many of the saints attest. But in relation to suffering, it is beneficial by empowering us to be at peace with not being in control. Many people have convinced themselves that they have a considerable amount of control in life. Although every person has some level by way of foresight, free will, and experience, God is truly in control. Mortification teaches us to stop depending on our own wants and designs because God is more important. When we are completely at peace with whatever God desires and allows to occur in our lives, we can withstand unimaginable sorrow and pain without losing hope or angrily blaming God or another.

The second inestimable practice which helps to prevent sorrow from expanding and suffocating us is custody of the mind. Perhaps custody of the eyes is a more familiar term and practice, whereby we combat the tendency of the eyes to lead us to sin through lust or curiosity. However, custody of the mind is an even more necessary practice. The mind is like a wild beast wandering about without control or submission. Most of us (if not all) struggle with unwanted thoughts. The mind is a most common place for temptations which come from the devil, from others, or from self. The devil can tempt us through our imaginations and memories. He can bring up sins or events of the past as a sort of temptation to sin.[112] The devil does not have the task of drawing our attention to one thing or another; the devil has the task of drawing our attention to anything but God. Whether it be the devil or our own weaknesses, the mind is a field of spiritual combat.

The mind is like a lawn. If the grass is unkempt and disordered, weeds, snakes, and ticks will infiltrate under concealment of the long grass. The lawn which is neatly kept and properly ordered is better protected from weeds and too short for snakes and ticks to greatly multiply. The weeds, snakes, and ticks are like the sinful

---

112   Though most people do not know, to find pleasure in one's past sins is itself a sin. This includes telling 'funny' stories to others when those stories include past sins. True contrition for sin does not allow for that sin to be the source of humor later in life.

thoughts. If we keep custody or guard over our thoughts and reject immediately the thoughts of doubt, hate, lust, presumption, judgment, dwelling in the past, living in the future, fear, pride, vanity, etc., then we prevent the thoughts from turning into sins. A sin must be *willfully* committed. When we have a thought but eventually dismiss it when we realize that it is inappropriate, we avoid sin. It is a tragedy how many of us are persecuted by our own thoughts because we feel guilty for having certain unwanted ones, feel powerless to overcome them, or we allow bad thoughts to wound, infect, and spoil our peace and spiritual lives.

Suffering is a particular cause of unwanted thoughts, and unwanted thoughts are a particular cause of suffering. For instance, when a husband says some flippant but stinging comment to his spouse, her internal turmoil causes her to reflect on it for a long period of time. These thoughts of revenge, sorrow, or betrayal are caused by the hurt. Also, these unwanted thoughts dwelling in the mind amplify bitterness of the grief and deepen the wound. This is an unfortunate and very common cycle which can easily lead to significant problems in relationships and individuals. Ceaseless complaining about trials and torments never yields relief, but more problems. As a general rule, dwelling on the past leads to depression; dwelling on the future leads to anxiety.

As harmful thoughts are allowed to marinate in our minds, they negatively affect our outlooks, perceptions, and dispositions. They increase the acuteness of the pain. Our souls tend to perceive fewer remedies, options, and outlets. We become tunnel-visioned in that there ceases to be a way out of our predicaments from this increasingly limited perspective. This is the lie and goal of the devil. Sorrow, stress, and pain can all weigh on our minds causing an increasing problem. When we replay in our minds a conversation or event of the past over and over again, we allow the past to consume us. The past should only be considered long enough to make the present less sinful by avoiding the same traps and conquering the same temptations.

When we constantly think that the worst thing will happen, we allow the devil to toy with our minds. We lack proper confidence in the providence of God because we judge the future with the grace of the present. This is a brief way to say that God gives graces as they are needed. For example, the person who thinks he cannot endure some agonizing pain another day or dwells on some potential tragedy that might occur...fails to trust that God will give the grace at that time to remain faithful and continue to bear the weight of the cross. This lack of trust must be an insult to God who gives us evidence of His generosity and love countless times throughout our lives.

The person who reflects on his or her inability to change (or help in) a given situation, chooses to focus on something of no benefit. Saint Thérèse of the Child Jesus once said, "If I did not simply live from one moment to another, it would be impossible for me to be patient, but I only look at the present, I forget the past, and I take good care not to forestall the future." All these thoughts which are allowed to grow and reproduce begin to increase torment and can even lead to depression and despair. So many people would be able to avoid drugs, medicines, and treatments if they would only learn to control thoughts.

God always offers a way out and a way toward peace. Custody of the mind is the answer. Keep watch over the thoughts of the mind like a shepherd keeps watch over his sheep. Custody of the mind combats these and many more potential problems by bringing our minds back to God. It is far better to reflect on Christ, Who controls all things, than to dwell on some situation in which we have no control. Herein lies a significant spiritual practice that dismisses temptations and prevents the 'domino effect,' which eventually results in a severe disturbance in our emotional, mental, or spiritual well-being.

Although keeping custody of the mind is a rather simple idea, it is also somewhat difficult because it requires great persistence. The mind is hard to control; do not allow failure to prevent peace and destroy success. To protect the mind, one simply ought to offer some simple and quick prayer as the unwanted thought enters the mind. For instance, "Blood of Jesus wash over me" is a simple and quick phrase that brings one's mind back to Christ.[113] This brief prayer is called an ejaculation because it is 'thrown out' at the moment of need. Instead of formally kneeling down to pray in a period of prayer, an ejaculation is short, sweet, and frequent prayer offered throughout the day. This prayer, or another ejaculation similar to it, ought to be used each and every time an unwanted or potentially dangerous thought creeps into the mind. This may occur a thousand times a day, which can be taxing; however, it is certainly worth the effort. Each of these thoughts become an opportunity for more prayer and the cause of turning our minds back to God. Suddenly, through this practice we can pray both more frequently and more regularly. Eventually, the annoyance and difficulty lessen as the practice develops into a habit. Undesirable thoughts become less effective and less potent.

---

113   Other examples: "Blessed Virgin protect me." "Holy Ghost inflame me." "May name of Jesus be praised." "Illum oportet crescere, me autem minui - He must increase, I must decrease." (John 3:30)....

Custody of the mind is a kind of armor in relation to suffering because it trains the mind to dwell on the things of God. In doing so, we keep ordered our minds, hearts, and souls by preventing the negative, dangerous and sinful thoughts from affecting us. In periods of difficulty, it is much harder to control our thoughts; nevertheless, if we develop this habit before or even in the midst of a trial, we are better equipped to move forward regardless of the weight of our crosses. Like a person who watches movies filled with blasphemy and sexual content is bound to be affected by the smut, the person entertaining negative or sinful thoughts is bound to be delayed or diverted from spiritual growth. These thoughts can even be mortally sinful. When we continue to remain vigilant by consistently flushing out and replacing those thoughts with positive and prayerful ones, we are bound to develop healthy mental and spiritual dispositions. As the mind considers and reaches out to God more regularly through this practice, God responds, blesses, and strengthens the soul by providing protection and healing as needed. Custody of the mind can also increase confidence in God, which is the fertile soil for hope to blossom.

Third, prayer is the oxygen of the spiritual life without which one cannot know or love God. Simply, it is loving communication with God. As any spouse desires to spend time with his beloved, so we ought to desire to spend time with God. Prayer is also a virtue; therefore, we must be willing to cultivate our prayer lives through repetition and consistency. Although all prayer is valuable for finding peace amid the turmoil, meditation is a specific type of prayer that helps in several ways.

Christian meditation as has been handed down from the saints throughout history is of great value. The new age movement and various eastern religions include methods and types of meditation; however, these are not methods of topic nor generally considered safe to practice because of the very different philosophies from which they come.[114] The Christian method is revitalizing and spiritually enriching. There are a few legitimate approaches to this form of prayer which are all helpful; however, Christian meditation in general is sufficient for the purposes of this book.[115]

Meditation is helpful in many regards: It refreshes our minds by removing self from the noise, distraction, and activity of society. It places our souls before God and provides an opportunity of intimate discourse. It makes our souls docile to the movements of the Holy Spirit. It pierces into the depths of the mystery of Sacred Scripture and Sacred Tradition. It applies the lessons and stories of the Bible to our lives. Although meditation rightly has numerous possible topics, for the purpose of enduring suffering and learning to use it for good by lovingly embracing it, the topic of the Passion of Christ is most profitable. Even if this is done only for five or ten minutes each day (or every other day), this is noticeably useful to implement.

The sufferings of Christ are far too numerous to count. Many of the difficulties and anguish He endured eludes the eye and human intellect. The depth of His love surpasses human knowledge; therefore, the depth of His suffering does the same. No person can ever exhaust the mystery of the Passion and death of Christ. A person who meditates on these pains daily for fifty years would still have never exhausted the depth of His strife. God is pleased and the Sacred Heart of Christ is consoled by frequent meditation

---

114   E.g. Centering prayer.
115   E.g. Ignatian method, Carmelite method, Lectio Divina...

on His Passion. The spiritual favors enumerated by many saints only multiply the many reasons to engage in this spiritual practice regularly.

In relation to suffering, meditation on the sufferings of Christ is so valuable because He instructs us in the way of virtues. Every virtue is made visible and implemented perfectly on the Cross. His patience, long-suffering, justice, temperance, liberality, humility, love...is exhibited in His torn flesh and His instructive words uttered from the Cross. The more we prayerfully investigate His torment, the more encouraged we are to suffer for love of Christ. The more familiar we become with the Passion of Christ, the more compassion we have for His pain, and the more passion we have to follow His example.

Through meditation, the Holy Spirit peals back the layers of mystery and leads our souls deeper into the Sacred Heart of Christ. The Divine Friend takes us by the hand to reveal the wonders of the love of God.[116] Our souls grow ever more familiar with this love which begins to draw out from us the desire for worldly allurements. Our soul's entitlement melts into gratitude, pride into humility, hardness of heart into compunction, and tepidity into a burning zeal to avoid sin at all cost. These meditations illuminate the sins and imperfections hidden in the depths of the soul. Christ's love draws out the poison of self-love from us. Saint John Chrysostom preached, "We should read our Lord's Passion constantly; what great benefit we will gain by doing so. Even if you are as hard as stone, when you contemplate that He was sarcastically

---

116   Ephesians 3:17-19: "...that you, being rooted and grounded in love, may have power to comprehend with all the saints what is the breadth and length and height and depth, and to know the love of Christ which surpasses knowledge, that you may be filled with all the fullness of God."

adorned; then ridiculed; beaten and subjected to the final agonies, you will be moved to cast all pride from your soul."[117] This love becomes ever more attractive and desirable. As two people spend time with each other, certain traits, quirks, and gestures tend to be passed to each other. Similarly, the qualities, riches, and purity of the love of Christ begin to shape the love and life of the Christian steeped in meditation. It is as if the love of the Savior is absorbed by us. Saint Bonaventure, an insightful and deeply educated saint, explained that the little knowledge he had concerning his theological insights came from his adoration and meditation on the Cross of Christ. He considered the crucifix to be "the book" that told him what to write.[118] Considering this saint is a doctor of the Church, his theological insight was certainly not little.

Jesus foretells the importance of this form of prayer: "And as Moses lifted up the serpent in the wilderness, so must the Son of man be lifted up, that whoever believes in him may have eternal life."[119] Those who are spiritually dying by the poison of sin need to faithfully and sincerely look to the Son of God lifted up on the Cross, like the Israelites looked at the serpent on the pole, and they will be spiritually healed. This look to the Cross is not an instant, but ought to be a life-long pursuit. Meditating on the death of Christ is a continual remedy for the havoc that sin causes to the soul.

Through consistent meditation, the sufferings of this life become more bearable because we possess more certain knowledge of Christ's nearness. Through meditation, the sufferings of this life become the means of resembling Christ more closely.

---

117   St John Chrysostom, Homilies on the Gospel of St Matthew, 87, 1.
118   St Alphonsus Liguori, Meditations on Christ's Passion, 1:4.
119   John 3:14-15.

This satisfies the growing thirst within our souls to follow Him. Through meditation, the sufferings of our lives become an exquisite form of prayer which purifies us of all desire for selfish gain. Through meditation, the sufferings of our lives become the 'litmus test' of our own sanctity. The heights of sanctity include a burning desire to suffer for love of Christ. Through meditation, the sufferings of our lives become innocent and pure gifts of love from our souls to God. Like the child who brings the bouquet of flowers to his mother to please her, so we are enthralled with adorning the Almighty with many presents formed out of our own small sacrifices, which imitate Christ's death. Meditation is an armor in that it converts our perspectives to the Catholic perspective. Rather, it changes our hearts into clay in the hands of the Holy Spirit, Who gives us the Catholic perspective. It enables us to view suffering not as an evil or an enemy, but as the stepping stones to greater holiness and the rungs on the ladder to Heaven.

Saint Paul famously teaches the importance of putting on the armor of God.[120] In addition to this armor of righteousness, truth, and faith, the spiritual practices of mortification, custody of the mind, and meditation prove helpful to encounter each and every kind of trial. Each of them stunt the growth of suffering and enable us to embrace the turmoil of our lives. Even more, we not only embrace our crosses, but use them as weapons against the evil one. The devil desires to use the wounds of our souls for ill purposes; therefore, this armor shields the soldiers of Christ from these attacks and trains us to conquer our foe with love. Only the Love of God in our souls can make something as repulsive as suffering an instrument of peace and joy.

---

120   Ephesians 6:10-18

PART 3
Our Examples:
Mary and the Saints

U p to this point we have discussed how to see suffering through God's eyes and examined the tools He has given us to transform our suffering. In Part 3, we will peek into the lives of some who have gone before us and chosen to deal with suffering in a holy way.

Thankfully, we do not have to suffer alone nor blindly. God has given us Mary and the saints as amazing examples of how to capitalize on the salvific power of suffering. In the following pages, we will see how Our Mother suffered more than any other human person throughout history and how her Seven Sorrows can bring us closer to Jesus through her. We will also learn to look to the saints as role models during our trials. Many of them suffered immensely, and there is much to gain by looking at their lives.

CHAPTER 14

Mama Knows Best

"As mariners are guided into port by the shining of a star, so Christians are guided to heaven by Mary."
—St. Thomas Aquinas

Instinctually, a child looks for his mother when inflicted with some wound or difficulty because in her he finds his source of comfort. God has created man to naturally seek help in trial. Christians ought to have an instinctual reaction, in temptation and sorrow, to turn to the Blessed Mother. God has given this holy and pure woman to every believer as a mother, guide, physician, and aid. Mary has been given a unique role in salvation history. She alone was chosen to be the mother of the Savior. She alone with Christ was conceived without original sin. She alone perfectly participated in His Passion and death. She alone suffered unimaginably with perfect resolve in her heart to give all to the Father as she stood at the Cross, the deathbed of her only Son.

There are many reasons to find refuge in the arms of Mary. Jesus found His consolation in her arms. The arms of Mary carried Jesus as a baby, kept Him warm, gave Him reassurance, and caressed His infant Body. As followers of Christ, Christians must learn to find consolation in the same arms that offered it to Him.

Our Lady of Perpetual Help is a title given to Mary because of her desire to aid all who pursue salvation. An icon scribed between the 13th and 15th centuries famously depicts Our Lady of Perpetual Help. The icon includes the archangels Michael and Gabriel holding instruments used for Christ's torment and Passion. Jesus, as a small child, is held in the arms of the Blessed Virgin Mary who is consoling her Son. The meaning of the depiction reveals that Christ was contemplating His future Passion by the instruments brought by the angels. So terrible was His contemplation, He ran quickly to His mother for comfort and security. He ran so fast, one of His sandals was broken and barely hangs on to the foot of the Savior. Although there is much more theology behind this icon, the image of Mary sweetly consoling her Divine Son clearly indicates how every Christian should run to her for assistance.[121] She is waiting. No other mother is able to provide the heavenly protection, care, healing, and comfort that the Queen of Perpetual Help provides.

Mary is the mother of all Christ's disciples. In the midst of His bitter anguish, Jesus looked down at His mother and His beloved disciple and spoke: "Woman, behold, your son!" Then He said to the disciple, "Behold, your mother!" And from that hour the disciple took her to his own home."[122] Mary is a woman of sinless and pure love of God. God created her and gave her more grace than any other human person. He designed His mother with unmatched beauty, splendor, and purity; yet, He has not held her for Himself. In a most generous act, God offers every follower of

---

121   Note Well: Is your relationship with Mary one of distance or intimate familial relationship? She is your mother; bring to her every problem, wound, trial and temptation you experience. You will find solace in her. You will find the help you need.
122   John 19:26-27.

Christ the marvelous gift and privilege to be sons and daughters of Mary as well. Her power, glory, purity, and motherhood are at the service of the common Catholic. Archbishop Fulton Sheen, a man who fought the enemies of the Church, wrote, "As the mother knows the needs better than the babe, so the Blessed Mother understands our cries and worries and knows them better than we know ourselves."[123] How could we not flee to her embrace? Mother Mary yearns to comfort the followers of Christ even as she yearned to comfort Christ. She honors and serves her Son by coming to the aid of her children.

As a result of the nearly limitless love with which Mary both served Christ and suffered with Christ, her reward in Heaven is inexpressible. Next to the humanity of Jesus, she is the most glorified creature. She is the Queen of Heaven who is exalted beyond all of the angels and saints. She has accumulated more treasure in Heaven than all other human persons combined. The way a flashlight compares to the sun, so the greatest of saints compare to the glory and splendor of Mary, the Mother of God. As Queen of Heaven, she is seated on the throne at the right hand of Christ, the King of all. From her position as queen mother, she has the ear of the King more fully than others. This situation parallels the relationship between Bathsheba, a wife of King David, and her son Solomon. She was asked to intercede on behalf of Adonijah to her son King Solomon, who claims he can refuse nothing to his mother.[124] Christ, also a son of King David, has given His queen mother

---

123   Sheen, Fulton, *The World's First Love.*

124   1 Kings 2:19-20: And the king rose to meet her, and bowed down to her; then he sat on his throne, and had a seat brought for the king's mother; and she sat on his right. Then she said, "I have one small request to make of you; do not refuse me." And the king said to her, "Make your request, my mother; for I will not refuse you."

to intercede for all her sons and daughters in the faith. Christ will refuse her nothing.

The victory of Mary is prophesied. She has a power over darkness that is not lacking. God has promised the victory over the ancient serpent to the woman and her seed.[125] This woman is the Blessed Virgin Mary and her seed is Jesus Christ. The devil knows his time is limited and the death and Resurrection of Jesus is his ultimate defeat. Therefore, he fears intensely the woman who gave the Son of God the human nature necessary to die on the cross. He fears intensely the woman who stood at His Cross with loving humility. He fears intensely the woman who continues to crush his head through her prayers and interventions in the protection of her children. Saint Bonaventure adds, "Men do not fear a powerful hostile army as the powers of hell fear the name and protection of Mary""[126] What evil or what trial is too big for the Lady who, by the power of God, will crush the head of the devil in the end?

Her absolute surrender in humility crushes the devil's prideful defiance. Saint Bernard encourages, "In dangers, in doubts, in difficulties, think of Mary, call upon Mary. Let not her name depart from your lips, never suffer it to leave your heart. And that you may obtain the assistance of her prayer, neglect not to walk in her footsteps. With her for guide, you shall never go astray; while invoking her, you shall never lose heart; so long as she is in your mind, you are safe from deception; while she holds your hand, you cannot fall; under her protection you have nothing to fear; if she walks before you, you shall not grow weary; if she shows you favor,

---

125   Genesis 3:15: "I will put enmity between you and the woman, and between your seed and her seed; he shall bruise your head, and you shall bruise his heel."

126   St. Bonaventure as quoted in Thigpen, Paul. *A Year with Mary.* Saint Benedict Press, 2013. p.62

you shall reach the goal""[127] With the help of this lowly virgin, even the worst suffering can be endured, even the most stubborn vices can be trampled underfoot.

Mary suffered more than any other human person to ever exist.[128] The depths of her sorrows and the heights of her bitter torment are unknown to even the holiest of saints in their entirety because her inner life is so profound. Mary's sorrows are proportional to her love. Because her love for God far surpasses natural understanding, her torments throughout her life are also a mystery. Certain qualities of her sufferings are worth mentioning:

1. **Her purity** increased her sensitivity to the pain. Sins dull the human experience of sorrow. Because Mary was without even a single sin, her soul was fully pure and far more sensitive to disorder, discomfort, and evil. The hideous irreverence, mockery, hate, and pride, with which her Divine Son was treated, forced the tip of the instrument of her torment to enter far more deeply into her Immaculate Heart. This indescribable bitterness washed over her time and time again.

2. **Her knowledge** was far superior to others. She knew more than any other human person the value and importance of her Divine Son. She loved Him with everything she was. She understood the terror of sin, many of its effects, the innocence and majesty of God, the reverence every creature owes Him

---

127   Saint Bernard of Clairvaux as quoted in Lancton, Fr. Thaddaeus, MIC. *Stepping on the Serpent: The Journey of Trust with Mary.* Marian Press, 2018.

128   Note Well: Jesus Christ is a Divine Person with a human nature. He is not a human person. Although He does suffer more than Mary according to His human nature, He is not a human person. Because He has a human nature, it is right to say that He is fully human as we are. However, who is He? the Son of God (Person); what is He? fully God and fully man (two natures Divine and human).

and more. So, the quantity of sin and abuse enacted against her Son expanded the degree of her torment beyond the comprehension of those who do not possess the same knowledge.

3. Mary bore her trials with **absolute resignation to the Will of God**. What she told the Archangel Gabriel at the moment of the Incarnation was an expression of the orientation of her soul throughout her life.[129] Mary never counted the cost of her service to God. As the devil said to God before the creation of humanity, "non serviam" [I will not serve], Mary lived out the direct opposite. She served, loved, and obeyed regardless of the personal grief incurred as a result. She recognized the lowliness of her human condition and thought of God alone. He is all she wants.

4. **Her sufferings** were such that only with the help of God could she bear them. Many spiritual authors maintain that she suffered more than all other human persons combined.

5. Mary's **unique intimacy with Christ** caused her to feel what He felt. Jesus Christ certainly suffered more than Mary; however, she did suffer immensely because of their singularly intimate relationship. Their mutual love was so strong and pure that they enjoyed unique and hidden knowledge of each other's sufferings. The Immaculate Heart of Mary and the Most Sacred Heart of Jesus are so united that both suffered together. A mother is cast into turmoil when she witnesses the trials of her child; so, the perfect mother was cast into unknown turmoil when she witnessed the immeasurable trials of her perfect Son. Father Frederick William Faber reflected, "She

---

129   Luke 1:38: And Mary said, 'Behold, I am the handmaid of the Lord; let it be to me according to your word.' And the angel departed from her."

lived in His Heart rather than her own. His interests were hers. His dispositions became hers. She thought with Him, felt with Him, and as far as might be, identified herself with Him. She lived only for Him. Her life was His instrument to be done with what He willed."[130]

6. **They caused each other an immense increase in suffering.** One of Jesus' principal torments was the knowledge that His mother endured so much suffering for Him. He saw clearly the sword tear through her spotless heart. Mary also understood that she was one of the greatest sources of torment for her Son.

"There was not one fresh indignity offered to Him, which did not pierce her soul, and make her bleed inwardly. As blows and blasphemies, insults and derision were multiplied, it seemed at each new violence as if she could bear no more, as if the sea of sorrow needed but another drop to break in upon the fountains of her life and wash them away in one terrific inundation. And yet she had to feel that the sight of her broken heart, ever before Him, was more dreadful to our Blessed Lord than the scourging, the crowning, the spitting, or the buffeting."[131]

The weight of His Cross was over-doubled by her sorrow. She became the chief executioner of her own Son in a way.

7. **Mary's sufferings were not limited to the days of Christ's Passion;** in a sense, she was always at the Cross. She has seven most notably bitter torments of her life. She lived under

130   Faber, Frederick William. The Foot of the Cross or The Sorrows of Mary, Refuge of Sinners Publishing, Inc. Pekin, Indiana, 2014. pg. 66.

131   Faber, Frederick William. The Foot of the Cross or The Sorrows of Mary, Refuge of Sinners Publishing, Inc. Pekin, Indiana, 2014. pg. 50.

the shadow of the crucifixion every moment since hearing the prophecy of Simeon.[132] Although she enjoyed a rich peace because of her purity of heart and Christocentric existence, she endured profound woes as well.

8. Her **sorrows were ever increasing** because the Holy Virgin continued to grow in holiness. Divine charity was growing within her. Her capacity to suffer increased along with her love for God. Thus, the quality of her torments were more richly felt with each passing day.

The Blessed Virgin's exceedingly broad and deep suffering make her the perfect companion to every sufferer. The Holy Mother knows precisely the torments encountered by every son and daughter she has. No trial or grief can elude her because she has suffered far greater. We possess the magnificent opportunity of bringing every wound and sorrow to the gentle hands of Mary. From the same hands, we receive consolation like Christ received food and water. Like a child who desires his mother to kiss his wound, we ought to bring every problem to the Queen of the angels. The consolation this gentle mother offers is one of many reasons to flee to her for refuge.

Additionally, suffering can influence and deepen our prayer lives. Through suffering, we better recognize the magnificent love of Mary at the foot of the Cross. For example, when a mother loses a child or a father witnesses the anguish of his daughter, the sharpness of Mary's agony is further revealed. Because Mary suffered so completely, every type of trouble and sorrow can aid the Christian

---

132   Luke 2: 34-35: "and Simeon blessed them and said to Mary his mother, 'Behold, this child is set for the fall and rising of many in Israel, and for a sign that is spoken against (and a sword will pierce through your own soul also), that thoughts out of many hearts may be revealed.'"

in his knowledge of his mother. As photographs and stories reveal to the children their mother's fashion, tastes, appearance, and past, so the torments of this life reveal Mary's sorrow, love, and humility to those of us who use our own pain to pierce into the mystery of Mary's life. Truly, every form of torment in this life can help us relate more closely and enter more deeply into the abyss of Mary's sufferings. Her soul is the mirror image of Christ crucified. O, how rich in grace are we who use our own trials to better appreciate and reflect on the trials of Mary. The Queen of Heaven said to St. Bridget: "I look around at all who are on earth, to see if by chance there are any who pity Me, and meditate on My Sorrows; and I find that there are very few. Therefore, My daughter, though I am forgotten by many, at least you do not forget me. Meditate on My Sorrows and share in My grief, as far as you can."

When we lovingly meditate on the sorrows of Mary, we give honor and hyper-veneration to her part in salvation history. All merit originates from Christ; however, her unequaled union with Him allowed her to merit more than all other Christians combined. Even in this generation, how many souls are converted, consoled, and blessed by her part in Christ's mission. Many graces are given to the faithful who meditate and reverence the Passion of Christ. Likewise, many graces are given to the faithful who reverence and prayerfully consider Mary's sorrows. Jesus Christ revealed to Blessed Veronica of Binasco, "My daughter, tears shed for My Passion are dear to Me; but as I loved My Mother Mary with an immense love, the meditation on the torments which She endured at My death is even more agreeable to Me."

Mary is capable of healing the wounds of the soul. A child expects his mother to console him and to heal him. We should have the same expectation of our heavenly mother by the power of God. The wounds of our souls need a spiritual medicine which has been given by God to the Blessed Virgin to treat the traumas and lesions made by sin and disorder. Children naturally learn to act and speak according to the parents' actions and words. They are more likely to manage with maturity various situations which are similar to those they witnessed maturely managed by their parents. Through consistent reflection on Mary's bitter torments, we begin to notice and even thirst for the perfect virtues with which Mary embraced her woes. These virtues are the colors of her immaculate soul, a masterpiece for all to admire. Through meditation, we thirst for the very same virtues employed by our immaculate mother.

Having enumerated a variety of reasons to suffer well and to devoutly approach the Blessed Virgin in all trials, in the next chapter we will entertain a brief exposition of the seven principal sorrows of Mary. We will identify how we ought to relate to her through suffering. These reflections are intended to reveal the direct connection between her sorrows and the many sorrows of her children.

CHAPTER 15

The Seven Sorrows of Mary

"From Mary we learn to surrender to God's Will in all things. From Mary we learn to trust even when all hope seems gone. From Mary, we learn to love Christ, her Son and the Son of God."
—*St. John Paul II*

T he devotion of the Seven Sorrows of Mary has been an aid to Christians for centuries. Mary endorsed and promoted this devotion through her apparitions to St. Bridget of Sweden in the fourteenth century. If we meditate on these seven sorrows, our hearts will be transformed, we will grow closer to Our Lady, and we will learn how to better handle and appreciate our own suffering.[133]

---

133   These reflections are born from personal prayer and study, not dogmatic teaching of the Church.

The First Sorrow

THE PROPHECY OF SIMEON

The Blessed Virgin Mary was the first to offer God the Father a truly dignified and worthy gift, His own Son. This moment was filled with joy as she fulfilled the ceremonial laws of Jewish tradition. She entered into the temple, the place where she spent years of her childhood in prayer and worship to God. This day, she entered with God in her arms. Christ was to be presented to God by Simeon the priest. The One for whom they have waited; the Savior has finally come. What greater gift could man give to God, than God Himself? As joyous as this occasion was for her, it also was the first of her heart-piercing sorrows.

Various Early Fathers believe that certain parts of Scripture are written in short-hand to avoid lengthy explanations of dialogues or events. It is very possible that Simeon actually explained in much greater detail the harsh trials that would pierce to the depths of her soul. Very likely, from her knowledge of the 'suffering servant' in Isaiah and other Old Testament prophecies, she may have foreseen a certain degree of Christ's Passion.[134] However, from this moment forward, Mary certainly understood to a great extent what her precious Child would soon suffer. The temple was the place of sacrifice where thousands of lambs were slaughtered each year. Mary brings the Lamb of God in her arms not to be slaughtered, but honored and presented to His Father. Therefore, it is poetic that the slaughter of the Lamb of God is foretold the first time He enters the Jewish temple.

---

134   Isaiah 53.

It is here that her great joy of being the mother of God was cast beneath the shadow of His impending death. This sorrow does not speak of a moment in time, but a relentless agony that followed her for 33 years. From this moment forward, the turmoil of anguish weighed upon her daily thoughts, as it did for Christ.[135] Was she reminded of the wood of the Cross every time He helped Saint Joseph cut and craft pieces of wood? Did she see with her mind's eye the nails in His hands every time He put His hand in hers? Did a knock at the door remind her of the knock of the nails that would be driven into His flesh? Did distant laughter in the streets transport her to the mockery of the soldiers? Though her precise knowledge is unknown, Mary suffered immensely as a result of the bitter cup of anticipation.

So many people suffer from a fear of the unknown. The parents of the son who goes to war, the spouse awaiting the results of a medical procedure, the father concerned about financial security, the mother considering the future of her handicapped child, the person worried about being accepted by others, the prospect of failure or embarrassment, the impending death of a loved one... These are simply a few common examples where anticipation continues to be a thorn of sorrow.

The first sorrow reveals an exceptional virtue of perseverance in the life of Mary. Perseverance is "the virtue by which one persists in the arduous good until the end is achieved."[136] As relentless as the sorrow of anticipation was in the thirty-three years of Christ's life, Mary's perseverance proved even more relentless.

---

135   Luke 12:49-50: "I came to cast fire upon the earth; and would that it were already kindled! I have a baptism [death] to be baptized with; and how I am constrained [anguished] until it is accomplished!"

136   http://www.sensustraditionis.org/Virtues.pdf

When people suffer without prayer, mortification, trust in God's providence, etc., they fail to implement the virtue of perseverance. Instead of offering these sufferings to God for spiritual growth, they just learn to live with them or try to drown them with distractions, medications, alcohol, or other false remedies. To use these sorrows as insight into the interior life of Mary and the dreadful anguish of her sorrows inspires further devotion to her. *She knows these sorrows and worse; she will help those who endure them.* Meditating on Mary's experience and profound torment of the first sorrow will aid us in carrying our crosses, help us to develop the virtue of perseverance, and cultivate in us a richer relationship with the Mother of God. *With Mary, there is peace.*

The Second Sorrow

THE FLIGHT INTO EGYPT

This escape, in the middle of the night, was a startling event for both Mary and Joseph. The lack of preparations, economic security, and the difficulty and danger of the journey were all components to the depth of this sorrow. The terrain and distance between Bethlehem and Egypt already ensured a challenging journey, which was greatly increased by the fact that the caravan included only one man with his wife and Child. Additionally, even in the youngest years of Christ's earthly life, Mary witnessed the Savior of the world rejected by His own people. The holy family had to escape from the hatred and envy of their own nation. The Savior was hunted by the ones He came to save. The King of Kings was chased by the chosen people of God. Mary knew with greater insight the majesty of this Child and the value of His Incarnation. Therefore, she experienced the terror of the situation in the depths of her soul. God was not even welcome in the very land He promised and set aside for His people. Mary and Joseph fled from their family, their culture, their language and even their temple, the central element and location of their worship in the Jewish religion. Furthermore, they were directed to flee to Egypt, the place of slavery for their ancestors. (The Israelites had been enslaved for 400 years by the Egyptians before God freed them and led them to the promised land.)

Regardless of the numerous prophecies, Scriptures, and stories that prepared the people of God to recognize the Messiah, they cast Him out and forced Him into the pagan nation of Egypt. The number of years the holy family dwelt outside of their homeland is uncertain; however, the sorrow of these years is certain. How many times did Mary smell the incense offered to false gods, see the statues of demons, and hear the prayers offered to idols, all while the living God was in her arms? What disinterest the people of Egypt must have had for the God-man living among them. Mary could not cease adoring her Son, while those around her only saw a foreigner and an outcast. Lastly, Mary knew the horror of Herod's actions.[137] How many women did she meet in her time in Bethlehem whose children were murdered by the command of this terrible ruler? What innocent blood was spilled in the pursuit of the Messiah. Her heart ached for those mothers, for those children, and for the souls of those who committed these heinous crimes against the innocent. The Catholic Church still remembers these innocent victims on the Feast of the Holy Innocents celebrated on December 28th each year. They are considered the first martyrs.

---

137   Matthew 2:16-18:

Many common sufferings are related to the woes of Mary in this second sorrow. For instance, those who suffer from rejection, past embarrassments, poverty, fears relating to safety, miscarriages, remorse for abortion, empathy for the losses our friends experience, witnessing the indifference of others towards God, loss of children in custody battles, etc., can all serve as a means to greater reflection and appreciation of the mystery of Mary's hardships.

This sorrow particularly illuminates the virtue of docility, which is the "ability to be led and take council from others."[138] She faithfully and rightly submitted to her spouse's guidance as he led them to and from Egypt. Ultimately, Mary was led by God in every moment of her life, which is the only reason she was able to embrace the excessive torments of her soul. To use our own torments as insight into the interior life of Mary and her dreadful anguish inspires further devotion to her. *She knows these sorrows and worse; she will help those who endure them.* Meditating on Mary's experience and profound torment of the second sorrow will aid us in carrying our crosses, help us to develop the virtue of docility, and enable us to cultivate a richer relationship with the Mother of God. *With Mary, there is peace.*

The Third Sorrow

THE LOSS OF JESUS IN THE TEMPLE

The precious child of Mary and Joseph was separated from them for three long days. According to Jewish practice, the men were expected to journey to the temple a few times each year. For at least one of the trips, the women and children would accompany the

---

138   http://www.sensustraditionis.org/Virtues.pdf

men to fulfill the laws of worship. On these journeys, the women and men would travel in separate parties of the same caravan. It is very likely that Mary and Joseph both believed Jesus to be with the other in the caravan. At the young age of twelve, He was alone in the city of Jerusalem while His parents traveled towards Nazareth.

In a single instant of realization, Mary's entire life was taken from her. Her whole being was centered on the Christ child. He is everything to her. To be without Him was to be without her heart. Mary and Joseph immediately separated themselves from the security of the caravan in pursuit of their Son. Without eating or sleeping, she sought Him for three days which felt more like three decades of loss and torment. She was exhausted physically, emotionally, and spiritually by this event. Mary likewise suffered for the sake of Joseph. As the man of the holy family, he was charged by God with the task of providing and protecting his spouse and Son. Her compassion for him in his sense of failure must have stung bitterly. Moreover, the third sorrow is uniquely filled with the anguish of confusion. Where was He? Why did this happen? Is it her fault? Did she do something wrong? Has His Passion already begun? Will He come back to her? Is Jesus taking back the rights of her motherhood which He gave her? How long before He is found? The profundity of this sorrow eludes Christians because of the immense love of Mary and the intimacy between her and Christ.

Finally, the tip of the sword of the third sorrow pierced the inmost recesses of her soul because Jesus was holding the sword. He chose to do this, to stay in Jerusalem, knowing the torment it would cause His parents. He is God, and He has the right, but why?

Although Mary had singular and deep insight into the mind and heart of Christ, God eclipsed her knowledge with the grief of the unknown. She was left without her Son and without her supernatural insight into His mind and intentions. When the opportunity arose after finally locating her Savior, she asked Him, "Why have you treated us so? Behold, your father and I have been looking for you anxiously."[139] His response is His first recorded words in Scripture: "How is it that you sought me?...[140] How could she do anything but search for Him? As naturally as the hungry search for food, the weary search for rest, and the lonely search for companionship, Mary sought for the 'apple of her eye' and the object of her heart. She searched for Jesus with all the energy of her little body and all the love of her great heart.

Many believe this sorrow to be the most painful. The fact that Christ chose this course of action and the obscurity of her insight into His interior life left her near desolation. Nevertheless, through exhaustion, anxiety, and confusion, she accepted it all and grew in holiness. She prayerfully "kept all these things in her heart."[141] She models the virtue of long-suffering. By this virtue, one is able to await the good. The measure of Mary's love lengthened the days into decades. For the heart sincerely and entirely devoted to God, separation from Him cannot be counted by minutes, hours, or days. Despite the duration of her turmoil, she pursued Him all the more. More than anyone, she knew what good it is to be in union with her Son. She would wait until the end of the world if necessary. Nobody but God could reduce her sorrow or satisfy her thirst for Him.

---

139   Luke 2:48.
140   Luke 2:49.
141   Luke 2:51.

Whoever experiences sufferings related to anxiety, difficulty in understanding Catholic teaching, difficulty in understanding God's ways, confusion about certain events or loss, lack of nearness to God, spiritual dryness, broken relationships, infertility, spiritual unrest, etc. can bear resemblance to Mary through them. To use them as insight into the interior life of Mary and her dreadful anguish inspires further devotion to her. *She knows these sorrows and worse; she will help those who endure them.* Meditating on Mary's experience and profound torment of the third sorrow will aid us in carrying our crosses, help us to develop the virtue of long-suffering, and enable us to cultivate a richer relationship with the Mother of God. *With Mary, there is peace.*

The Fourth Sorrow

MARY MEETS JESUS ON HIS WAY TO CALVARY

Mary encountered Christ as He carried His Cross. She saw Jesus with the instrument of His torture, the altar for His sacrifice. This journey through the inner city of Jerusalem to Golgotha, the place of the skull, was ridden with pain. The exhaustion of every muscle and the ache of every part of His Body was exacerbated in this lengthy journey. He fell at least three times while He walked through the streets displayed as a worse-than-common criminal and an enemy to the people. Mary accompanied her Son on many journeys to Jerusalem and other locations; this day she accompanied Him to His death.

This sorrow is the first which Mary must endure without the strong, holy, and humble aid of Saint Joseph. At least in the others, she had a stalwart support and companion with whom to suffer.

The Holy Catholic Church wisely directs the attention of the faithful to this moment amid the several horrifying events of the Passion. Mary suffered every part of the Passion and death with Jesus. However, in this sorrow, they shared a specific moment of mutual anguish, mutual understanding, and mutual empathy, in a special way as they met on the road.

They looked into each other's eyes in this brief moment; they gazed into each other's soul. The weight of the Cross, the flagellated flesh, the deeply wounded shoulder, the words of mockery, the heartless laughter of the onlookers, the cruelty of the Jewish priests, the physical exhaustion, the lack of food and sleep, all accumulated into an overwhelming torment for her dear Son. Yet, these external sufferings did not compare with the internal strife caused by His love for humanity and the cost of His mercy. He saw every sin of the past, present, and future, and was affected by them. He knew it all, and she knew Him.

Mary saw that the unrecognizable condition of His Body only manifested the worse condition of His soul. She knew better the real breadth and depth of the sufferings of the Savior. While others only noticed His torn flesh, she noticed His tormented heart. This knowledge and her love for Him made His torments her own. The internal condition of His soul revealed to her the condition of her own. Her heart was the mirrored image of His.

During the few moments between Mary and Jesus on the road to His crucifixion, they shared a lifetime together. Among all the people there, only these two had a clear grasp of what was occurring, the value of His life, the value of His death, and the measure of sorrow that accompanied it.

The extraordinary sorrow of Mary was a suffering for Christ that outweighed those torments mentioned above. Mary's insight into this reality is what caused one of her deepest wounds. Unimaginable and inexpressible strife pierced every part of her soul because she knew He suffered immeasurably more because of her. His pain was doubled because she suffered so greatly. She was the cause of the heaviest weight of the Cross of Christ up to that moment. Father Faber calls Mary the "executioner in chief" as a result. He wrote, "The sight of her face at the corner of that street had been worse a thousand times than the terrible scourging at the pillar. It was her face which had thrown Him down upon the ground in that third fall."[142] Her sorrow was the sword which tore through His heart. Her knowledge of this was the sword which tore through hers.

Therefore, the Blessed Mother manifests the virtue of meekness. Amid all the horrific blasphemies, the ridicule and irreverence toward the Messiah, Mary never struck back. Not a single word of scolding, not a single action of revenge ever emerged from her perfectly meek soul. Meekness is the "moderation of the delight of vindication." By this virtue one is capable of overcoming that thirst for vengeance and the temptation of anger. Peter imperfectly loved Christ and was willing to attack the soldiers who came to arrest the Divine Master. Mary perfectly loves Christ and was unwilling to lash out at those who mercilessly put Him to death. Through meekness she accepted the will of God, even to the extent of witnessing her own heart nailed to a tree.

---

142   Faber, Frederick William. The Foot of the Cross or The Sorrows of Mary, Refuge of Sinners Publishing, Inc. Pekin, Indiana, 2014. pg. 50.

Those who experience sorrow from empathy for friends, the injustice of taking advantage of the poor, the injustice of rape or abuse of the innocent, and the injustices of war and violence, all have a way to relate more effectively to the fourth sorrow of Mary. To use them as insight into the interior life of Mary and her dreadful anguish inspires further devotion to her. *She knows these sorrows and worse; she will help those who endure them.* Meditating on Mary's experience and profound torment of the fourth sorrow will aid us in carrying our crosses, help us to develop the virtue of meekness, and enable us to cultivate a richer relationship with the Mother of God. *With Mary, there is peace.*

The Fifth Sorrow

MARY STANDS AT THE FOOT OF THE CROSS

Finally, Jesus' time of crucifixion and death had arrived. He had willfully come to the place of His final torment. Without a moment's respite, the soldiers began to attach His sacred limbs to a tree. In the Garden of Eden, a serpent led humanity into sin from a tree; on Mount Calvary, Jesus led humanity to God from a tree.

Any mother would be horrified and inconceivably distraught by witnessing the sight and sounds of her child being brutally affixed to a cross with nails, lifted up, and slowly drained of life as His body is pulled by gravity and His lungs crushed by the weight of His own body. How much more the mother who loved her Son more than any other mother? How much more the mother who knew distinctly and felt personally the agony of her Son?

The nails which attached Christ to His Cross were the same nails which were driven into her heart. Fr. Faber notes the falling of the hammer was not one event; rather, each knock of the nail was a "separate martyrdom".[143] Jesus was lifted up on a Cross when He should have been exalted on a throne and given a crown of gold, rather than thorns. Only Mary properly reverenced and dignified the Lord of Lords with her perfect adoration. Where the thorns pierced His brow, she had covered Him in kisses. Where the nails tore through His feet, she had covered with sandals. Where the nails pierced His hands, she had covered with her own hands. She had given Him this Body, that now dripped with His Sacred blood. The Holy Spirit gave Him His human soul. Both are in utter anguish. The Blessed Mother felt this anguish as if His Body was still a part of her own.

In addition to the horrors of Christ's sufferings, Mary was pierced by the loss of salvation of those involved. Judas, one of the twelve, had betrayed Christ and refused to seek forgiveness.[144] If only he would repent and know the mercy of the Savior. She must have been reminded of Judas when the thief near Christ began to mock him without remorse. Unlike Saint Dismas, the thief who repented on the deathbed of his own cross, the other seemingly failed to accept the eternal life offered by the One hanging on the Cross next to him. Because Mary is in perfect union with God, she thirsts for the salvation of souls with great intensity. Even the prospect of losing one of her potential sons or daughters to the ancient serpent is a source of pain.

---

143   Faber, Frederick William. The Foot of the Cross or The Sorrows of Mary, Refuge of Sinners Publishing, Inc. Pekin, Indiana, 2014. pg. 325.

144   John 17:12: "While I was with them, I kept them in thy name, which thou hast given me; I have guarded them, and none of them is lost but the son of perdition, that the scripture might be fulfilled."

Likewise, the Mother of Jesus suffered extraordinarily because she could not follow her Son to the grave. She submitted to God's Will in all things, even in surviving her only child. Father Faber reflected: "It must be remembered also that there was a peculiar grief to our Lady in not dying with Jesus, which we cannot appreciate, but only contemplate far off. Union with Jesus was so habitual to her, and union of so close and vital a nature, that it had become her life; and now, in the most important act of all, she was not to be united with Him. She was to differ when she most longed to resemble Him...never scarcely was she more intimately united with Him than when she let Him go without her."[145] How could she go on living when her whole life was dying? How could she remain here when her only desire was leaving? Only God could give her the strength.

The greatest suffering for Mary in this sorrow was the greatest suffering of Christ, that is the dereliction of the Father. Christ cried out from the Cross, "My God, My God, why hast thou forsaken me?"[146] Though the extent of this darkest torment of the Savior eludes even the greatest of theologians, it cast anew the full humanity of Jesus into the agonies of desolation. Father Denis Fahey remarks, "In virtue of His union with us, because we form one body with Him, Our Lord saw Himself laden with sin in the sight of His Father."[147] Most likely, this sorrow was so devastating, not even His mother could follow the full distance into the depth of His Passion. Nevertheless, she writhed with pain because of her

145   Faber, Frederick William. The Foot of the Cross or The Sorrows of Mary, Refuge of Sinners Publishing, Inc. Pekin, Indiana, 2014. pg.49.
146   Mark 15:34.
147   Fahey, Denis. The Social Rights of Our Divine Lord Jesus Christ, the King. Loreto Publications, 1932.

greater insight into His desolation and the causes of it. The suffering of Mary at the Cross is simply above and beyond the ability of any other disciple of Christ to understand. For thirty-three years her union with Him flourished in order to make the maximum amount of suffering possible in these hours. What fiber of her being was not drenched in bitter anguish? What other suffering could possibly be added?

Throughout each moment and every new wave of horror which washed over this Blessed Mother's heart again and again throughout this salvific event, she remained patient. The virtue of patience is "the ability to suffer evils well."[148] Mary never abandoned her Son or shrank from her rightful place there at His side. She never surrendered to her near limitless grief or retired from her motherhood. She stood at the foot of the Cross. She stood stalwart against all the evils perpetrated against her Child. She stood tall even as the sword found its mark in her soul. The perfect exhibit of the virtue of patience is manifested in Christ's embrace of the Cross and Mary's humble compassion next to it.

The crucifixion entails so much suffering that all personal strife and grief can find some relation to it. However, some are more easily related. For example, those who suffer with long battles against alcoholism, drug abuse, habitual sins, terminal illness, death in general, post-traumatic stress disorder, forgiveness, the priest scandals in the Church, the state of the Church, inability to help loved-ones who suffer greatly, coming to grips with old age and physical and mental limitations, etc., can find greater appreciation of the sufferings of Christ. In doing so, we raise our eyes again and again to the Son of God lifted up like the bronze serpent. Little by

---

148   http://www.sensustraditionis.org/Virtues.pdf

little, God removes the poison of internal disorder, restores to life the decaying parts of the soul, and converts suffering into sanctity. Furthermore, to use these sufferings as insight into the interior life of Mary and her dreadful anguish inspires further devotion to her. *She knows these sorrows and worse; she will help those who endure them.*

Meditating on Mary's experience and profound torment of the fifth sorrow will aid us in carrying our crosses, help us to develop the virtue of patience, and enable us to cultivate a richer relationship with the Mother of God. *With Mary, there is peace.*

The Sixth Sorrow

JESUS IS TAKEN DOWN FROM THE CROSS

Once the Roman soldiers determined the 'spectacle' was complete, Mary watched the sacred Body of Christ continue to change colors and grow colder as the loss of life manifested more apparently. "It is finished."[149] Jesus would suffer no more in this life; however, Mary's sufferings continued. This sorrow is particularly concerned with the treatment of His Body and her loneliness.

The Roman soldiers intending to quicken the death of the criminals broke the legs of those near Christ. Because various signs of Christ's Body indicated death, they wanted certainty. Callously, the Roman soldier stabbed the lifeless Body of Jesus. The Body of Christ purchased eternal life for the world. His Body is the vehicle by which humanity could be brought into right relationship with God once again. Yet, this invaluable and most precious relic was treated with so much apathy and disdain. Piercing His side was

---

149   John 19:30.

just another task for the Roman soldier before he could retire for the evening. For Christians, the spear that pierced Christ's side is the key of Heaven; it was to ascertain His death, but it poked a hole in the floor of Heaven and salvation flooded down. To Mary it was a jolting event that sent a wave of terror throughout her body and soul. The sound and movement of His Body must have been imprinted into her memory when the soldier shoved the spear into it. An angel once told St. Bridget, a mystic especially devoted to the Passion of Christ, that so great was the shock to our Lady in the moment His Body was pierced that only a miracle saved her from an instantaneous death from grief. How many times she saw Him heal with those hands, preach with those lips, comfort others with those arms, draw near to the outcasts with those feet. How could someone so precious be maltreated so completely? If ever the phrase "to cast pearls before swine" perfectly explained a situation, this was it.

The spear that ripped through His Body tore open His silent and ravaged heart. Blood and Water flowed.[150] This is the water used in the Sacrament of Baptism, the first sacrament, the entrance into the life of God. This is the Precious Blood of Jesus which is made present in the Sacrifice of the Mass and consumed for the salvation of the world. The Eucharist is the highest of the seven sacraments and the summit of sanctity. Therefore, the other five sacraments and the whole life of the Catholic Church is found between these two sacred liquids. A preview to the salvation which they promised is visible in the conversion of the soldier who pierced His heart. With poetic beauty, the sinner opened the Heart of Christ where Blood and Water pour out; the same Blood

---

150   Luke 19:34.

and Water is used by the Catholic Church in the sacraments to bring the sinner into the heart of Christ. She witnessed this Water and Blood gush forth from the Body of Christ and give life to the infant Church.

Mary was blessed to care for Him the first nine months of His earthly life in her womb. She was blessed to care for Him the next thirty years. The right fell to her to care for Him one last time. She is blessed to prepare His Body for burial. It was for her to cleanse the bloodied flesh, to wash the dirt from His face, to ring the Blood from His hair, to remove the thorns from His brow, to readjust the patches of flesh which hung down, and to wrap His naked Body. Many times she had combed His hair, cleaned His face, and straightened His clothes in His childhood. As these images emerged in her memory, the stark contrast of His cold flesh, His bluing lips, and numerous injuries concealed His naturally attractive appearance. The love and reverence with which she fulfilled this duty must have atoned for so many sins against the Body of Christ. While preparing His Body for burial, did images of the outrages against the Body and Blood of Christ that would be perpetrated by priests in mortal sin or irreverence and sacrilegious Communions through the generations of the Catholic Church amplify her sorrow and increase the love with which she treated His Body in this task?

The clearest form of torment in this sixth sorrow was perhaps her loneliness. She no longer has her Son to accompany her in her woes. Now nobody on earth knows the measure of her grief, the state of her soul, or the beauty of her interior life. Again, the great joy of Mary's relationship to Christ was eclipsed by separation from Him. The imperfections and hardships of earthly life are difficult, but imagine how much more difficult it would be for a person who experienced the majesty and splendor of Heaven for three decades in her own home. Earth would be a sort of hell for that person. Mary's relationship with Jesus was the nearest image and experience to Heaven that is possible; therefore, the separation she experienced was the closest experience of hell she could have. Simeon's prophecy was fulfilled to the syllable; the sword penetrated her entire being.

Any person who has spent even the slightest amount of time investigating the life of Mary and cultivating a devotion to her, recognizes her humility. She radiates the virtue of humility, which is a "willingness to live in accordance with truth" and to not judge oneself greater than he is."[151] Humility is the queen of virtues and necessary for spiritual growth. It acknowledges the majesty of God to the extent of making everything about Him. It disregards one's own desires for the sake of fulfilling God's will in all things. The devil, who succumbed to pride would not serve God (non serviam). Pride caused the devil's fall into the abyss from his former place of glory. Humility is the cause of Mary's elevation from the pit of strife and ridicule at the foot of the Cross to the highest place of glory among all angels and human persons in Heaven. True humility is not self-abasement or self-hatred; it is to accurately understand one's lowliness in relation to God's grandeur. Therefore, submission to God in all things and at all times is its effect. Saint Bernard taught, "The three most important virtues are humility, humility and humility." Even when God's will includes terrifying torment as in the case of Mary, humility accepts it all and prefers to suffer greatly than to reject God's will. Through this

---

151   http://www.sensustraditionis.org/Virtues.pdf

virtue, a person finds fulfillment and peace only in fulfilling the will of God. In this state, the turmoil and grief of earthly existence fail to separate humble souls from peace, because embracing it is part of God's will at that time. Few virtues are as necessary as the virtue of humility in properly accepting suffering and transforming it into a great spiritual value.

Secondly, humility is a shield which prevents suffering from causing many bad effects within the soul. Human sorrow naturally can lead to feelings of defeat and hopelessness. These feelings lead to the very dangerous sin of indifference toward the spiritual life. Humility teaches the Christian to continue striving because union with God is all that matters in life. Indifference fails to see the grandeur of God and reason for seeking Him above all things. Humility prevents this blindness and leads to a greater desire to please God than to please self. A poem by G.A. Studdert Kennedy, which envisions Christ coming to modern-day America, tells how indifference causes Jesus greater pain than He endured on Mount Calvary:

When Jesus came to Golgotha, they hanged Him on a tree,

They drove great nails through hands and feet, and made a Calvary;

They crowned Him with a crown of thorns, red were His wounds and deep,

For those were crude and cruel days, and human flesh was cheap.

When Jesus came to Birmingham they simply passed Him by,

They never hurt a hair of Him, they only let Him die;

For men had grown more tender, and they would not give Him pain,

They only just passed down the street, and left Him in the rain.

Still Jesus cried, "Forgive them, for they know not what they do,"

And still it rained the wintry rain that drenched Him through and through;

The crowds went home, and left the streets without a soul to see,

And Jesus crouched against a wall and cried for Calvary.

Those who suffer from loneliness, rejection, having been the victim of cruelty, having witnessed their loved ones maltreated, having witnessed the mistreatment of the Eucharist, the abuses of the Liturgy, or the indifference toward relics and holy objects, all share some relation to the woes of Mary's sixth sorrow. To use these sufferings as insight into the interior life of Mary and her dreadful anguish inspires further devotion to her. *She knows these sorrows and worse; she will help those who endure them.* Meditating on Mary's experience and profound torment of the sixth sorrow will aid us in carrying our crosses, help us to develop the virtue of humility, and enable us to cultivate a richer relationship with the Mother of God. *With Mary, there is peace.*

The Seventh Sorrow

THE BURIAL OF JESUS

After all the appropriate preparations had been made, Jesus' Body was laid in the tomb. As other times in the life of Christ, Mary was reminded of His childhood. There seemed to be a parallel in certain ways between the beginning of Christ's life and the end of it. For example, Christ was laid on the wood of a manger at birth; at death, He was laid on the wood of a Cross. He came into the world without any clothes, and He left the world without any... The seventh sorrow of Mary shares in these parallels. She laid His Body and fixed the burial garments just as she had laid Him in the manger and swaddled Him with clothes. Did she make for Him the burial garments as she had made for Him the garment with which He was swaddled? It is nearly certain that these similarities and many others were not lost on Mary. They most likely caused her greater grief.

Clearly, the three days of separation from Christ as Mary pursued Him restlessly in the third sorrow, is paralleled with the seventh. However, in the seventh there is a completion to Mary's desolation. The previous sorrows find a culminating end at the tomb. Mary was separated from Christ again for three days, but she had not the benefit of searching for Him. At least in the third sorrow she had the prospect of reaching Him and embracing Him. In this sorrow, she had nowhere to go, nobody to seek, no duty to perform for her Son. In the third, there was an ignorance that God allowed to overtake her. She did not understand why Christ remained in Jerusalem; however, in the seventh, she knew all of it. She knew where He was and why He was gone. What is it to be beyond the reach of consolation? The seventh sorrow leaves her even without this much.

All that was left was for her to make the journey back, reliving His tortures, seeing again the drops of Blood left in the street, on rocks and even on the sandals of the spectators. The closing of that tomb shut her off from the last physical connection she had with Him. With the previous sorrow, she had the consolation of caring for His Body, reverencing this instrument of salvation. The seventh leaves her with nothing. Mary's soul was not attached to even a single earthly comfort. She belonged to Christ alone. Physically, He had left her too. There is no limitation to the darkness of a world without Jesus.

The apostles, Mary Magdalene, and others were very familiar with Mary. They must have seen such holiness in her. They must have seen such resemblance to Christ. The most natural act for them would have been to remain near her these three days. She is the mother of consolation. Though they suffered a tiny fraction of her woes, she sought to care for them. Like the loving mother who still cares for her child while ill, Mary gave consolation to others while she was suffocating in her internal torment. She never resented them for their sins, which crucified Christ. She never resented them for abandoning her Son at His death. Her kindness was unbounded and little known by those who received it.

Mary teaches all Christians the importance of kindness in suffering. Generally, suffering causes us to turn inwards. We think of only our own strife. We forget about other people and believe others should be considerate of our conditions. The Blessed Virgin reveals that kindness is a most valuable form of healing in suffering. When we combat self-love in order to serve another in need, we resemble the Queen of Heaven. She forgot herself entirely as she served others. The Mother of God made herself the servant of others despite her far more piercing sorrows. She gives herself as the role model for all who suffer. She exhibits kindness as an ointment which opens the suffering soul to the healing power of God.

Kindness brings us out of ourselves; it forces us to recognize the reality beyond the points of our anguish.

Those who endure despair, depression, painful memories, desolation, difficult responsibilities in caring for others, sense of things falling apart, sense of uselessness, helplessness, lack of control, etc., can find greater insight into the seventh sorrow of Mary by applying these sorrows to one's meditation on the entombment of the Body of Christ. To use these sufferings as insight into the interior life of Mary and her dreadful anguish inspires further devotion to her. *She knows these sorrows and worse; she will help those who endure them.* Meditating on Mary's experience and profound torment of the seventh sorrow will aid us in carrying our crosses, help us to develop the virtue of kindness, and enable us to cultivate a richer relationship with the Mother of God. *With Mary, there is peace.*

The Seven Promises of Devotion to the Seven Sorrows

The Blessed Virgin Mary understands deeply the injuries, hardships, and wounds of her children. The Lord has given her to all of us as a mother and a queen to guide and protect all who recognize her unique role in salvation history. Each of us ought to flee to her for refuge and find in her all the strength necessary to use suffering as an instrument for good. Through her example, her nearness to Christ, and her intercession, the devil's attempts to make suffering the fall of the Christian and the disruption of internal peace is thwarted. Through every torment she continued to rightly recognize the love of God. She kissed, caressed, nurtured, clothed, carried, protected...her little Child for years. This is precisely what she does spiritually for her children to this day. Through her sufferings she became more Christlike. All must draw near to this holy woman and she will teach them and help them to do the same. Her entire life is a road map to sanctity and a model for suffering well. By her side, every single child of hers prevails over sorrow, sin, and satan. One ought to stand at her side as she stood by Christ's. She is the 'Star of the Sea' by which we ought to navigate through the turbulent waters of suffering to arrive at the throne of the Prince of Peace.

Suffering in the hands of a person who knows how and where to direct it with humble and pure love, is like a paint brush in the hands of an artist adding another layer to the masterpiece, or the chisel in the hand of a sculptor removing another layer of marble, causing the emergence of the final product. The hands of the Blessed Virgin are the place to commend your sufferings. She is the artist, the sculptor, the teacher, the master, and our Mother. She is the only one next to her Son who suffered perfectly. Mary has the 'Midas touch;' everything she touches is perfected. Therefore, we ought to lend her our pains and she will turn them into precious gifts with which to adorn the Most Holy Trinity.

Saint Bridget received seven promises which are granted to every person who prays seven Hail Marys each day in honor of the seven dolors of Mary. The promises are as follows:

1. "I will grant peace to their families."

2. "They will be enlightened about the divine Mysteries."

3. "I will console them in their pains and I will accompany them in their work."

4. "I will give them as much as they ask for as long as it does not oppose the adorable will of My divine Son or the sanctification of their souls."

5. "I will defend them in their spiritual battles with the infernal enemy and I will protect them at every instant of their lives."

6. "I will visibly help them at the moment of their death — they will see the face of their Mother."

7. "I have obtained this grace from My divine Son, that those who propagate this devotion to My tears and sorrows will be taken directly from this earthly life to eternal happiness, since all their sins will be forgiven and My Son will be their eternal consolation and joy.

CHAPTER 16

Look to the Saints

"If God sends you many sufferings, it is a sign that He has great plans for you and certainly wants to make you a saint."
—*St. Ignatius Loyola*

G od has seen fit to manifest His glory in the lives of his creatures. He does this in every creature to some degree; however, this is magnified in the lives of those who have free will. Man has the ability to choose, serve, and love God in a way that animals, plants, and inanimate creatures cannot. By way of love, man manifests the goodness of God in a radically visible way. In the lives of the saints, which are lives filled with suffering and death, the power of love over hate and faith over fear is made visible. As the stars light up the dark sky of night and reveal the majesty of God, so the lives of the saints illuminate God's glory in the darkest of conditions and reveal His presence. They expose the ability of God to act in and through the lives of those who give themselves to Him, regardless of the opposition and difficulty of their situations. They unveil the hidden works of God through their sufferings and trials.

The holy men and women of the past should not be seen as distant and remarkable people who bear little relation to those who live now. Their lives are not simply ancient models of extremely virtuous souls whose ability to help others ended with their death. Rather, the saints are intimately united to all who live in the state of grace. Grace binds us to God; it also binds us to the community of God. Baptism is not only an entrance into the family of God whereby a sinner is made into a son or daughter of the Most High. Baptism is also an entrance into the community which Christ constructed, the Holy Catholic Church. This community extends beyond the reach of death and unites those in Heaven with those who are in Purgatory and on earth. Love of neighbor and service to others is not ended at death. Those in Heaven still offer prayers on behalf of those fighting for their salvation on earth. Therefore, the saints are the brothers and sisters of all the faithful. Grace binds each one to the others. By the Blood of Christ, the saints are deeply related to everyone living in the state of grace on earth. Furthermore, they continue to aid their brothers and sisters in multiple ways: their example, their graces, and their intercessions.

The devil aims to convince each of us that we suffer alone. That we suffer needlessly. That we suffer unjustly. As suffering increases and continues, it is more and more difficult to see God's goodness and aid. The devil or our own ideas can lead us to feel victimized. As we begin to believe that we are mistreated by God or the universe, we revolt against faith, trust, and love. We reject the only source of hope and learn to hate the God Who loves immeasurably. Many of the practices and virtues mentioned throughout the previous chapters combat these tactics of the evil one. Staying close to the saints is another immensely helpful practice.

The saints teach all who investigate their extraordinary lives that no measure of suffering is too much for those who trust in

God. They dispel the lies of the devil. We can focus so much on our own troubles that we believe we suffer more than anyone else. We think we are in unique situations. This false notion can become an excuse to not move forward, to leave behind our prayer lives, or to give up altogether. As false as it is, it can be a debilitating reality that casts us into a world of hurt. God wants more for us and makes Himself available to satisfy our every need. The lives of the saints reveal to the world, generation after generation, that nobody is alone; God is active and near. They illuminate the steps to Mount Calvary because they have walked in the footsteps of Christ. By their examples, they take us by the hand and lead us to the Savior. It is an invaluable gift to find so much suffering, loss, and turmoil in the lives of those who continued to advance spiritually and were undeterred by the impediments to peace. Their heroic examples are forever a testament that suffering does not have to be an obstacle to holiness or profound joy. Their actions and endurance testify that suffering is not an indication of God's absence or lack of love for His creatures, but an indication that His love is stronger than any and all earthly hardships.

Whatever difficulties arise, the life of some saint or another is applicable and helpful. Any person who seeks success is in need of a goal, a target at which to aim. The lives of the saints disclose this target by making visible the qualities and virtues necessary to cultivate in order to move forward. They instruct us on how to shape our perspectives, actions, and mentalities to Christ. To dwell on Christ is to climb toward Heaven by focusing on the One who heals and saves. To dwell on our own trials and torments is to remain fixed on ourselves, and we can neither heal nor save. The saints set their focus on Christ without falter. The model of their lives continues to teach, all who listen, the secrets of spiritual growth and serene joy.

As mentioned above, God created humanity in a very connected way. Sin affects countless people in unperceived ways. Likewise, grace affects countless people in unperceived ways. God is able to take the loving action of some Christian and apply its value to people in other generations. The good the saints have accomplished in their lives continues to affect the Christians of today. This reality is visible in certain ways. For instance, the courage and efforts of the many priests and religious who came to the Americas to evangelize have given an invaluable gift to all who are raised there. They have access to a society which at least accepts Christianity. In a similar way, God is able to take the graces they merit through their loving service and apply it in various ways to various people in various eras as He sees fit. Grace flows downstream like a river to quench their most fundamental thirst, which is their thirst for God. Grace continues to affect and aid people in their need. Saint Thérèse said, "How often have I thought that I may owe all the graces I've received to the prayers of a person who begged them from God for me, and whom I shall know only in heaven." Only in Heaven will it be revealed how certain actions, prayers, and acceptance of suffering benefited numerous others by God's providence. Although the saints no longer live on earth, their merits of the past and prayers of the present continue to bless the people who do.

The saints continue to aid people through their intercessions. The saints long to have relationships with their younger brothers and sisters who have not yet completed their pilgrimage toward Heaven. Those who study the lives of the saints generally experience in one way or another how certain ones call out to them. How helpful it is to realize that God has sent others to be with us in our trials. Along with a guardian angel, the saints offer their continued support as they intercede for others. The Little Flower remarked, "When I die, I will send down a shower of roses from the heavens, I will spend my heaven by doing good on earth."

Every Christian ought to ask for these intercessions and trust in their generosity. They continue their acts of love as they walk with those who are in need. The white-robed army of holy ones, who give glory to God Almighty at every moment, belongs to the faithful by right of grace, as their companions and friends in every trial.[152]

Job

The book of Job in the Holy Bible is most applicable. Any book which offers advice and a proper perspective on suffering without incorporating the book of Job is remiss. This inspired work acknowledges God as truly and wholly just in all His ways. Job is an extremely righteous man who has a comfortable life, financial security, and a large and healthy family. However, God offers Job an even greater reward if he remains faithful through a terrible and lengthy trial. The devil seeks to destroy Job's righteousness by inflicting horrendous suffering. Job's children are killed, his livestock are destroyed, and he is subject to abject poverty. Later, he develops a tormentous skin disease. His own wife wants him to curse God for his problems; he will not. His three friends try to convince him that he is unrighteous and the cause of all his problems. Although Job holds firm at first to his own justification, he

---

152   Revelations 7:9.

eventually acknowledges that God can do all things according to His will. He submits to God in all things. From this surrender comes his peace and the restoration of his blessings. God makes His glory known as He remarks, "Where were you when I laid the foundation of the earth? Tell me, if you have understanding. Who determined its measurements..."[153] Job is rewarded greatly for his fidelity. He becomes richer than before and grows his family considerably. He lives a long life and is able to enjoy multiple generations of his family. Job teaches everyone who suffers that God has a plan and desires to only increase the blessings He offers to His children.

St. Lidwina

Saint Lidwina is one of many remarkable women who suffered intensely before reaping everlasting reward. Like Job, she can inspire anybody to use suffering as a tool to greater purification and sanctity. To see an innocent woman experience so many problems for so many years, while persistently offering them for the salvation of souls, is an encouraging history which should continue to shape the spiritual lives of Christians to this day. Father Remler gives a concise account of her life of prolonged suffering:

> "This saint was born in a little town of Holland in the year 1380. In her youth she was possessed of great beauty, on which account she was eagerly sought in marriage by several young men. But she, enlightened by grace, spurned the world with its false pleasure and resolved to dedicate herself exclusively to the service of God by embracing a life of virginity. That her

---

153   Job 38:4-5.

natural beauty might not prove a danger to her virtue, she begged of God to deprive her of it. Her prayer was heard.

"In her fifteenth year while out skating one day in company with several companions, she fell on the rough ice in such a manner as to break a rib in her right side. This marked the beginning of a long train of sufferings which were to last without interruption for no less than thirty-eight years. An abscess formed in her side which defied the skill of the best physicians, and in the course of time became the source of an infection which spread over her body. For some years she was able to move about, though only with considerable difficulty and pain; but the last thirty-three years of her life she was completely bedridden. Her sufferings increased as time went on. Gangrene appeared in the wound in her side and continued to spread. It was the source of intense pain, especially during the last seventeen years of her life, for she was no longer able to move any part of her body except her head and one arm. Nor was this the extent of her sufferings. Besides the pains caused by sickness, she had to endure the bitter pangs of great poverty, especially during the winter season. Moreover, she suffered greatly from calumny, false suspicion, and harsh treatment at the hands of those who considered her an impostor.

"While in the beginning she experienced considerable difficulty in perfectly resigning herself to the Divine Will, she soon learned to suffer with the most perfect disposition when at the advice of her confessor she made the bitter Passion and Death of Our savior the constant subject of her meditation and received Holy Communion as often as her condition permitted. These two means enabled her to endure the pains of her long illness not only in a most patient manner but also with a wonderful joy and gladness. After having thus been a victim of undeserved sufferings for the long space of thirty-eight years —from the age of fifteen to fifty-three—she dies a happy and peaceful death in 1433."

Pope Leo XIII recognized her as a role model for every Christian and highlighted her heroically virtuous life as worthy of veneration when he canonized her in 1890.

St. Louis and St. Zélie Martin

The final example is unique in that it involves a married couple who embraced their crosses together. Saints Louis and Zélie Martin, the parents of Saint Thérèse of Lisieux, were both pious Catholics who discerned a life devoted fully to God. Eventually, they both came to the realization that God called them to the vocation of Holy Matrimony. Through His grace, they found each other. They had a happy and holy marriage together as they centered their family on God and instructed their children in the ways of prayer.

Beginning in the year 1865, their lives were submerged under the loss of loved ones. Saint Louis lost his father. The couple lost a one-year-old son in 1867. The year 1868 proved to be a challenge when a second son passed at the age of one as well. Saint Zélie's father passed away the same year. Additionally, in 1870, their daughter Hélène died at the age 5 and their daughter Mélanie died only two months old. Later, Saint Zélie suffered from breast cancer and passed away while her youngest child Thérèse was still only a few years old. Her father was left to care for the remaining five girls who survived the trying times. He was without his faithful companion who walked with him throughout their trials. His daughters began joining the convent (in time, they all became religious nuns). This included his 'little queen' Thérèse who joined at the age of fifteen. Losing her to the convent at such a young age was considered one of his greatest trials. From his heart emerged these words, "Thérèse, my little queen, entered Carmel yesterday. God alone can exact such a sacrifice, but he helps me mightily so that in the midst of my tears my heart overflows with joy." Eventually Saint Louis's mind deteriorated to the point of needing care from an institution. He died in the odor of sanctity in 1894.

Through their sorrows and losses, these two holy souls prevailed in faith. Their lives are fossilized in human history as evidence of the power of God's consolation and the resilience of the faithful Catholic. With their lives, they explain to every other person that God is present in suffering. This fidelity is an encouragement to every soul to find the fortitude to embrace the cross. Their example is not by their own doing, but by the grace of God. This same God who made them beacons of sanctity desires to make every person a saint forged in the fires of His Divine Love. "What then shall we say to this? If God is for us, who is against us?"[154]

There is much to learn from Job's example and the examples of the saints. Whatever suffering we encounter in our lives, there is a saint to help us through. Compiled on the next page, is a list of some saints and their sufferings. I hope it inspires us to delve into the lives of the holy ones who have gone before us. It is not an exhaustive list by any means, but one to get you started on your search:

---

154   Romans 8:31

Saint	Suffering(s)
St. Alphonsa	Death of parents, burned, illness, weakness
St. Anthony Zaccaria	Death of a parent, illness
St. Apollinaris	Beaten, tortured, martyr
St. Augustine Zhao Rong	Religious persecution, tortured/martyr
St. Bega	Runaway, isolated
St. Benedict of Nursia	Isolation
St. Birgitta of Sweden	Death of mother, Death of spouse, visions
St. Camillus de Lellis	Absent father, mother died, gambling, wounded
St. Dymphna	Death of mother, murdered by her own father
St. Elizabeth of Portugal	Family strife, war
St. Hedwig	Difficult marriage, infertility, death of a child
St. Ignatius of Loyola	Knight, injured, sea travel
St. John Eudes	Plague, lived in a barrel
St. John the Baptist	Beheaded, martyr
St. Junípero Serra	Infection, physical impairment
St. Kateri Tekakwitha	Smallpox, scarred body, eye damage, persecution
St. Margaret Ward	Prisoner, martyr
St. Maria Goretti	Death of a parent, stabbed/murdered
St. Mary Magdalene	Possessed, witnessed Jesus' crucifixion
St. Maximilian Kolbe	Sent to Auschwitz, sacrificed himself

St. Monica	Husband and son were not Christians
St. Padre Pio	Stigmata
St. Stephen of Hungary	Death of a son in a hunting accident
St. Thomas the Apostle	Doubt, martyr

All saints have suffered in some way. I pray that this list inspires you to do more research on the saints. There is much to learn from them.

CONCLUDING
THOUGHTS

The existence of strife and sorrow is not an indication that God does not exist. It is not an indication that God is cruel. Rather, it indicates that God loves us enough to give us the ability to choose Him. Sin is the ultimate cause of suffering. Yet, God is not deterred in His desire to draw us to Himself and fill us with His sublime glory. He is the loving Father who guides His faithful to the gates of Heaven and extends His glory to them. Suffering is not our enemy but "the straight and luminous ladder by which we mount to Heaven."[155] For the faithful, it is a mechanism by which God is able to lead us to conversion, remit our temporal punishment, and provide us with greater eternal reward.

God answered the problem of Adam and Eve's sin with the response of the Incarnation (God became man). He answered the problem of eternal punishment with the death and Resurrection of Jesus Christ. His power is such that even the worst of sins and the worst of suffering can be transformed into the greatest of blessings. Imagine what He can do with your sufferings if you let Him.

---

155   Martinez, Luis. *True Devotion to the Holy Spirit.* Sophia Institute Press. Manchester, New Hampshire, p.205.

We have examined how the loving Father uses our trials to draw us out of sin, purify our souls, remit temporal punishment, bestow grace on others, and merit Heavenly reward. We have explored various gifts of God which provide the necessary strength and grace to take up the cross and cherish it as the key to unlock the gates of Heaven. By practicing the theological virtues, frequenting the sacraments, implementing the practices already discussed, and learning from the saints, suffering is harnessed into a weapon against which the devil and all the forces of evil are powerless.

We have not however, exhausted all of God's generosity. This book merely contains a fraction of His benevolence. An exposition of the seven gifts of the Holy Spirit, the loyal help of a guardian angel, the power of sacramentals, and the effects of the other five sacraments are just a few of the unmentioned manifestations of God's abundant love. The Holy Spirit will use your sufferings to purify your soul and multiply the heavenly splendor that awaits you. God be praised, even in our sorrow, *especially* in our sorrow!

Lastly, entrust your entire life to the pure hands of the Blessed Virgin. She is your mother, given by God as a most helpful gift for your sanctification. She knows your pain and she wants to console you as she leads you along the journey toward her Son. Consecrate your life to her and she will place you in the Most Sacred Heart of Jesus, where peace and joy are endless.

Ave Maris Stella

Ave maris stella,
Dei Mater alma,
atque semper Virgo,
felix caeli porta.

Sumens illud Ave
Gabrielis ore,
funda nos in pace,
mutans Hevae nomen.

Solve vincula reis,
profer lumen caecis
mala nostra pelle,
bona cuncta posce.

Monstra te esse matrem:
sumat per te preces,
qui pro nobis natus,
tulit esse tuus.

Virgo singularis,
inter omnes mites,
nos culpis solutos,
mites fac et castos.

Vitam praesta puram,
iter para tutum:
ut videntes Iesum
semper collaetemur.

Sit laus Deo Patri,
summo Christo decus,
Spiritui Sancto,
tribus honor unus. Amen.

Hail, O Star of the ocean
God's own Mother blest,
ever sinless Virgin,
gate of heavenly rest.

Taking that sweet Ave,
which from Gabriel came,
peace confirm within us,
changing Eve's name.

Break the sinners' fetters,
make our blindness day,
Chase all evils from us,
for all blessings pray.

Show thyself a Mother,
may the Word divine
born for us thine Infant
hear our prayers through thine.

Virgin all excelling,
mildest of the mild,
free from guilt preserve us
meek and undefiled.

Keep our life all spotless,
make our way secure
till we find in Jesus,
joy for evermore.

Praise to God the Father,
honor to the Son,
in the Holy Spirit,
be the glory one. Amen